Chris,

Always Lead with PoP!

Power Of Positive
Leadership

Chris,

Always lead with love!

[signature]

Power Of Positive Leadership

POP Leadership

Scott A. Benning

ISBN: 1542982316
ISBN 13: 9781542982313
Library of Congress Control Number: 2017902053
CreateSpace Independent Publishing Platform
North Charleston, South Carolina

Dedication

This book is dedicated to the many who have developed me into the person I am today. Family always comes first, and therefore, this is for the love of my life, Cheryl, who has shaped me—more than she will ever know—into someone who desires to live a positive life with our amazing sons, Scott "Anthony" Jr. and Jason, and our daughters-in-law, Darcie and Brianna. They have made us proud grandparents to our little men, Cole and Hunter, and our princesses, Evelyn and Gracelyn.
Of course, this is also for my parents, Lester and Kathleen Benning, who gave me and my five siblings life and raised us to be loving people. I am proud to be a Benning and grateful for the good times, bad times, and—most of all—fun times that shaped me early in life.
And for Cheryl's parents, Elvin and Betty Taylor, who gave her life and raised her to be the wonderful person she is— full of love and the desire to always serve others. They have been a fountain of support throughout our life together and continue to guide us through their example.
This book is dedicated to my navy family too. If you have served in the US Navy long enough, you understand the term *navy family*. During my thirty-year career, I spent more time with my navy family than I did with my actual family.
Lastly, I want to thank my puppies, Cody and Molly, who taught me every day, unconditional love and loyalty. I sometimes

wish we could all be more like our dogs in that we would
then truly understand serving to make others happy.
I thank you all—and thank God most of all for
allowing me to live my life with all of you.

Acknowledgments

THERE ARE SEVERAL people I need to thank, as they helped me to develop the Power of Positive (POP) Leadership and this book. First is my dad, Lester Francis Benning. During his fight with cancer, I thought sharing POP Leadership with him and asking him to review my material would help him to maintain a positive focus. He had been a leader, both professionally and in his personal life, for many years. I think it did help him, but the cancer was too strong; God took him home in 2008. Not a day goes by that I do not think about the impact he had on my life. It was important for him, in the last year of his life, to show all his family that he had lived in service of God and others. He watches over me now, and I can feel his touch in my soul every day. I love you, Dad.

I also need to thank my shipmates on USS *George Washington*. While I was your command master chief, you all taught me more than you will ever know. Led by Captain Martin Erdossy III and Captain (now Rear Admiral) Dee Mewbourne, we were the greatest crew to ever sail the seven seas. Captain Mewbourne reviewed my material and helped me to understand the concept of a tipping point and its role in cultural change as expressed in Malcolm Gladwell's book *The Tipping Point*. Furthermore, Captain Randy Peirson, who was our chief of staff at Navy Region Mid-Atlantic at the time, provided his perspective on my material and kept me focused on the importance of what I was doing. Thank you all for your guidance in developing POP Leadership.

Finally, thank you to the following trusted agents: my sister, Cherie Haller; my shipmate, Master Chief Petty Officer of the Navy Rick West; my close friend, Loren Linscott; and my two sons, Anthony and Jason, all of whom reviewed my content to ensure it was relatable to readers of all kinds. I so appreciate your help and support in expanding the reach of POP Leadership to a much larger audience through this book.

Contents

INTRODUCTION

Life Is a Learning Journey

Life is a learning journey on which you will pass through many destinations. How will you remember the destinations, and how will those you encounter at these destinations remember you?

–Scott Benning

I created this quote to encourage those in attendance at speaking engagements to begin a reflection of their past experiences. This enables them to discuss the concept of learning from the past, their understanding of positive energy, and how they can focus on applying positive attributes to their future.

A true leader understands that if he or she wants to continue to foster success, his or her personal learning process cannot stop. Leaders who don't understand that their personal learning process cannot stop often find themselves in very bad situations. Even so, each situation you encounter in a leadership position constitutes a journey of learning new ideas, practices, and skills so that you can then apply them to future situations—not only to achieve success for yourself but to replicate it with others too.

Admittedly, it took me a while to get to a place where I could put my words into a book. I have spent some time with the concept of POP Leadership, all the while giving my material and thoughts away to others so that they could teach and talk about it. Why? Leadership is about sharing your experience with others to enable their success. I have never considered POP Leadership a means of self-promotion or a way to create a revenue stream. The concept is about promoting a positive atmosphere and focus in the navy I served by sharing with others how a change in perception could improve their leadership approach.

When you feel the need to take credit for something, people will see you as less than genuine. Leadership is about giving credit to those you lead, the ones who are actually accomplishing the work and mission. After I retired from the US Navy, many of my shipmates enabled me to further learn about leadership by requesting that I come to their events and speak about POP Leadership; they even suggested that there was a need for me to put my journey into words to facilitate their continued learning after my brief time with them. Similarly, I felt there was a need to expand my lessons outside of the navy. I had watched corporate America and noticed how, over time, some companies struggle as they forget what made them successful in the first place.

Success does not come through any type of sales concept; rather, it comes through people and how those people—the leaders of any given organization—serve their customers. It is often not the product you are selling that makes you successful. In fact, more times than not, it is a positive personal experience that brings people back to you. It is my hope that this book will turn many organizations onto this thought process, thus making them realize that any new level of success comes from returning to the old methods that led to their initial success. It comes from never forgetting your principles and using such concepts to meet the needs of those you serve and lead. For it is the people—not the structures or the continual expansion of products—and the careful execution of all their roles that makes the difference. Serving those who desire to return to you after a positive life experience is the key to continued success.

So, why should you read another leadership book and why should you read *my* thoughts on the topic? I have learned a great deal in my study and execution of leadership, and I offer a rare perspective derived from the opportunities I took as I rose through the enlisted ranks of the

US Navy to ultimately become one of its top five senior enlisted leaders. Moreover, during those thirty years of service, I came to understand the importance of the many relationships in my life and how each one of them played a role in developing me into the person I am today.

Rank Understanding

For the many who may not understand the military rank structure, here is some basic information. Each service has an officer and an enlisted group of leaders. Officers are appointed authority and their assignment by congressional approval. The enlisted force serve for periods of time to do the day-to-day mission work. I guess you could say the officers are the white-collar work force and the enlisted group are the blue-collar work force. However, as the years progressed, the officer corps began to realize that the experienced senior enlisted leader would be of great value in training enlisted and junior officer sailors, to the benefit of the navy's future.

My time in the navy was spent in the enlisted ranks, which start with the pay grade I received as an E-1, or a Seaman Recruit. The enlisted ranks progress to E-9 as follows:

- E-2 Seaman Apprentice
- E-3 Seaman
- E-4 Petty Officer Third Class
- E-5 Petty Officer Second Class
- E-6 Petty Officer First Class
- E-7 Chief Petty Officer
- E-8 Senior Chief Petty Officer
- E-9 Master Chief Petty Officer

Many master chiefs stayed in their technical rating to lead and develop that force of sailors, and their jobs were critical to our overall success. Some master chiefs pursue command leadership positions and become command master chiefs to be the senior enlisted leader in their commands. They are just as important as their technical counterparts and assume more responsibility.

The command master chief route is the one I chose; I was fortunate to be selected as master chief after only fifteen years of service. When I reached sixteen, I went on my first command master chief tour in Fighter Squadron One Zero Three (VF-103). I was there for only two years, but the carrier air wing commander of CVW-17, Captain Dana Potts, had taken notice of my leadership abilities in the squadron. He called me to his office and asked me to be his next command master chief for the entire eight-squadron air wing—a very humbling honor. I deployed on board USS *George Washington* in 2000 while in VF-103 and then again in 2002 as the CVW-17 command master chief. After only two years at the air wing, I was selected—even having served only twenty years in the navy—to be the command master chief of the USS *George Washington*. The aircraft carrier is one of the most challenging sea duty positions for a command master chief, and, as you will see, I learned a great deal from this experience.

To add more details to my position, the command master chief ranks have many layers. Today, we have command senior chiefs who become command master chiefs. Of the 287,000 enlisted force, only 1 percent become master chiefs. And of that 1 percent, only 700 become command master chiefs. The tiers continue as some are selected to fill seventeen force master chief positions across the navy and then four fleet master chief positions. Finally, one leader is chosen to be the master chief petty officer of the Navy and the senior enlisted leader to the entire navy.

My tours as a command master chief included VF-103, CVW-17, USS *George Washington* (CVN 73), Naval Station Norfolk, Virginia, and Navy Region Mid-Atlantic. I ultimately became the fleet master chief of manpower, personnel, training, and education for the entire navy and directly supported the chief of naval personnel.

It might also interest you to know that the command master chief directs the chief petty officer's mess in his or her command. The commanding officer oversees the entire unit, the executive officer is second in command, and they are both also considered the leaders in the wardroom. As a group, the commanding officer, the executive officer, and the command master chief are often referred to as the command leadership triad. The three work closely together to communicate with and train their crew while readying them to meet the combat missions assigned.

The Need to Create a Positive Culture

During my last eight years in the US Navy, I started to notice that our leaders were focusing on the very small percentage of negative situations generated by a very small population of sailors, officers and enlisted alike. And these sailors were responsible for their various situations. Do not let my words confuse you—we have the finest leaders and sailors in our navy, and I was proud to serve for and with those great Americans. All the same, as elected officials and other outside sources scrutinized the very small percentage of negative situations, our leaders needed to apply specific attention to these matters to ensure that they were addressed. They were forced to ensure that such situations did not grow in number while also managing the public perception of the many who served. However, focusing on only the negative aspects of the navy while addressing its whole population, most of whom are continuing to be successful, can affect the culture of the entire organization and turn it into a negative environment. As the US Navy is a very large organization, its leaders need to be delicate in their approach.

In 2007, I was the command master chief for the country's largest naval base, Naval Station Norfolk. While there, I once found myself at a chief of naval operations all-hands call, in a room of over three hundred senior enlisted leaders and officers. During this event, I told the navy's most senior leader about my concerns over our leaders focusing on the small percentage of negative issues within the organization. I told him that such issues were created by fewer than half of 1 percent of our sailors, and that addressing everyone as if they were all part of the problem was, in my view, creating a negative environment.

A chief of naval operations all-hands call is when the US Navy's senior leader visits various areas to not only provide information about changes in policy but also—and more importantly—gain perspective from sailors throughout the organization. It is a tremendous opportunity for the leader to listen, learn, and lead. These three words—*listen, learn,* and *lead*—were on a bumper sticker that the then chief of naval operations (CNO), Admiral Mike Mullen, used to communicate the importance of leaders' listening to the sailors and civilians they were commanding and thereby learning from them. He also expressed his desire for all leaders to continue to develop personally and professionally through reading and schooling. In my view, he expected them to exercise leadership as servant leaders, who serve those they lead instead of having those they lead serve them.

Admiral Mullen was and is a great leader, but I felt the need to confront him with my concern that we were focusing our energy on the smaller damaging population rather than the 99.5 percent of sailors who were doing wonderful work every day to support and defend their nation.

During this all-hands call, a young officer asked Admiral Mullen about what he perceived to be a deteriorating standard of conduct within the young enlisted sailors. Admiral Mullen responded that he had also seen a deteriorating standard; he went on to say that it was an issue at all levels and that all leaders must take ownership of the problem. At this point, I could not merely sit down and listen to the discussion, so I stood up. Admiral Mullen recognized me and asked if I had something to add. I responded politely, saying that I respectfully disagreed with the young officer's and the admiral's assessment. The points I made included the fact that fewer than half of 1 percent of sailors were involved in the situations being discussed and that we spent a great deal of our time discussing negative issues versus celebrating the noble work being conducted by 99.5 percent of our people, who were performing with honor. I went on to state that maybe those who could not live up to the US Navy standard should be directed to leave the organization and that we should begin to reinforce positive behavior. If we did this, maybe the half of 1 percent would realize that they needed to perform or move on. Some in this world will seek attention in any manner; if making a destructive decision can help them to get it, that may be what they choose to do.

Much to his credit, Admiral Mullen took my comments and turned them into a positive point: he insisted that we needed to challenge all our sailors and keep them on the path to success. So clearly, even the best of leaders can be set on a negative course if no one "course corrects" the conversation.

I have no idea what became of that young officer, but I hope he learned a great deal from that discussion. Admiral Mullen, on the other hand, eventually went on to become the chairman of the joint chiefs—the highest military rank in the US Department of Defense. I discovered many things through watching Admiral Mullen, including his compassion for service members and their families. He led with considerable wisdom and experience, and always with the aim of serving by obeying the constitution that established our great nation. I will never forget seeing him at the burial service for a young corpsman who had been killed in action while Admiral Mullen was the chairman of the joint chiefs. You could see and feel the sadness this man endured for his sailor and the family he had left behind. The admiral's compassion for people was strong.

Joe Campa was the Master Chief Petty Officer of the Navy at the time of my interaction with Admiral Mullen, and he was with the CNO at the all-hands call. He thanked me for my comments after the session. He then went back to his office in the Pentagon and had his staff document the number of punishable issues in proportion to the population. He and his team confirmed that fewer than half of 1 percent of the sailors engaged in any sort of destructive behavior.

As I departed the all-hands call with the CNO that day, I knew I could not just stand up and discuss my concerns; I had to take action to change the culture myself. This session was the catalyst that led to my creation of the Power of Positive Leadership. It became both a training program and a speaking platform as I continued to rise through the ranks. I still use it today, not only to teach it to others but also in my efforts to listen, learn, and lead!

It Takes Only One to Change the World

It takes only one person to change the world. When I developed POP Leadership and shared the concept with my two sons, Jason, the younger one, told me I needed to see a video. He directed me to the music video for Nickelback's "If Everyone Cared." I encourage you to view this video for the inspiration it can provide. Once I had seen it, I was overwhelmed and told Jason that I was not trying to change the world, just the culture within the US Navy. He said, "It starts with one, Dad. And you are trying to change the world." This was an amazing and humbling sentiment coming from my then seventeen-year-old son. Of course, I had worked to prepare both my sons for life by encouraging them to read leadership books. But having my son view my actions in this manner was still very rewarding.

I am extremely proud of my family. Cheryl, who was my high school sweetheart, has been a beaming light of positivity that helps our family to navigate the path to success. Our two sons now work as leaders in the navy and continue to develop in a positive manner. Scott "Anthony" Jr. is the US Navy civilian director of fitness, sports, and aquatics at the world's largest naval station, and Jason Christopher is a surface warfare officer in a riverine squadron and leading sailors. Each member of our family has a leadership role, and we often talk about leadership and learn from one another.

I hope you find the same type of support through your relationships that I have within my family. It is important to discuss leadership with those closest to you—in both your personal and professional life—on a daily basis. Engaging in such communication is how we reflect, learn, and develop, and if you get nothing else from reading this book, please know that my intent is to hopefully inspire you to continue to do just that. How will the people you meet at your many destinations in life remember you? Always put your family first and go forward with a positive attitude. I believe they will then remember you as a fulfilled leader.

As you read the remainder of this book, seeking my perspective on leadership, please keep in mind that life is a learning journey. It is my hope that you can learn to apply the Power of Positive Leadership to your personal and professional life. Promote a positive culture by inspiring, challenging, and empowering the people around you. You deserve to live a happy and satisfying life, and so do those you live and work with, superiors as well as subordinates.

I have included POP points at the end of each chapter for you to consider. It is my hope that you will also review them with the people you lead as they too read the book to spread the Power of Positive Leadership.

Some chapters may include recommended reading at the end that relates to the topic at hand. I have also included, in appendix A, a list of the leadership books that have helped to shape me into the leader I am today. Reading is fundamental to all that we do, and I hope that you will find some of these sources useful in your leadership development. Also, in appendix B, I have added reflection questions that reiterate the many questions I ask you to consider throughout the book. You can use them daily for your own self-reflection. Pick one question each day and acknowledge that reviewing that question may just give you and your team the opportunity to grow through the Power of (your) Positive leadership.

I wish you only the very best on your journey, and I know that if you work hard to apply the many thoughts and principles discussed in this book, you will become a successful and fulfilled leader. Give everyone your very best, and always lead with POP! Yes, it does take only one person to change the world. If you do not feel that you can change the world after reading this, I know you *will* feel that you can positively change someone else's world—and a global change always begins with changing one thing. I ask you to seek ways in which you can pay your positive energy forward—even if those ways are outside of your comfort zone. The Power of Positive Leadership works only if you first exercise it yourself and then teach it to others, so that it can be replicated. Are you the one who will change the world? I think you are. Read and lead with POP.

CHAPTER 1

Creating a Positive Culture: Attitude, Approach, and Atmosphere

MARK AND READ the following section each day, prior to your leadership reading.

Daily Read

Good morning! Are you smiling, and are you ready to start your day by having a positive impact on those you lead and follow?

I ask that you start each session of reading this book with this paragraph. You may ask, "Why is this necessary?" First and foremost, I want you to do some self-reflection and put yourself in the proper mind-set every day before you begin to read. This is very important, as it is my experience that, no matter where you are in the hierarchy of the organization you serve, you *can* change the environment and the overall culture that currently exists there. By looking at yourself first, prior to looking at others, you will gain a new appreciation for the value you bring to the lives of everyone around you. If you fail to recognize your own potential, then you are likely contributing to any problems that may exist in your environment. Be a part of the solution. Enable those you work with, and even those you work for, to make the most of you and everything you have to offer. Your attitude and how you approach each relationship, and each task, impacts the outcome of your group's character.

Never forget the impact of one. It starts and ends with one, and you are that one. Until you realize this, you will always be part of a negative environment. Only you have the potential to turn it into a positive one. Wake up each morning grateful for the opportunity to make positive change. Make sure you are assessing every day to determine whether there was more you could have done the day before and what you will do today to make self-improvements so that you can then help others to improve. Smile at yourself first, and be proud of who you are and who you are working to become. You can only be proud of others if you can first feel pride within yourself that grows your self-confidence that enables you to develop others. Becoming the one begins with believing in the one. You are the one, and I believe in you.

Realizing How Your Approach Can Change Others' Attitudes (Kill Them with Kindness)

I have learned a great deal from many leadership authors who have helped me to shape my attitude and how I approach each day. These authors, who I will routinely refer to, have found a way to connect with their readers and promote the understanding and acceptance of a leadership concept. I hope that I can do the same with you through my own stories.

President Abraham Lincoln was known as a great storyteller. It was his remarkable ability to connect with any group that enabled him to become the fifteenth president of the United States and arguably the most popular president in our young nation's history. Being able to relate to others allows you to understand what motivates them and what they appreciate. Abraham Lincoln knew that it was his responsibility as leader to understand and connect with others, not the other way around. He was in his position first and foremost to serve our nation and its citizens. His people did not elect him so that they could serve him. This is a very important perspective to evaluate.

You may say, "Well, I am not the leader of my organization." And I would argue with that assessment. In my experience, an organization reflects its leaders at the head of the team. But I also know that every member on that team is, in fact, a leader. Whether you are the most junior or the most senior member of the organization, you have the ability to influence both decisions and outcomes at various levels. Therefore, you also have the ability to influence the atmosphere and overall culture for your team.

For instance, this occurred during my recent trip to a local department store. The young lady at the cash register had the ability to influence my future behavior. As I approached the register, I watched her interactions with other customers. She was rude and unsupportive of the customers' needs. How would this sort of behavior impact your decision as to whether you would shop at this store in the future? I realized I had the ability to improve her environment by utilizing a tactic that a great leader and friend of mine, Captain Martin Erdossy III, had taught me. He called it *kill them with kindness*.

Captain Erdossy had been the commanding officer aboard USS *George Washington* and had selected me to be his command master chief. On an aircraft carrier, the air wing operates and maintains the airplanes. The squadrons airplanes and personnel are not permanently assigned to the ship until the overseas deployment begins. This can be a hectic time as the ship becomes very crowded and new relationships are established. Some spaces are assigned to the embarking air wings when the ship is built. Over time, however, as air wings embark and disembark from the ship, something called ship creep occurs. This is when the permanently assigned ship's company personnel start taking over air wing spaces and use those spaces for something other than maintenance. When the new air wing arrives, the ship's company personnel desire to keep the spaces they have taken. As you can imagine, this creates a great deal of friction between the two groups because the air wing personnel then feel like they have to fight to get their spaces back so that they can perform their part of the mission.

Captain Erdossy's approach to this situation was to kill them with kindness. On our carrier, we had to understand that we were providing the air wing a service so that they could operate the weapons system as a team. Captain Erdossy and I had the ability to bring the entire team together at the beginning, to shape their attitude and the overall atmosphere with our accommodating approach. If we did our part to create a positive environment, it would produce a successful team—and a six-month-long deployment would be enjoyable rather than one burdened by arguments over many minor issues.

So, I adopted Captain Erdossy's approach with the young lady at the department store register. I understood that maybe she was having a bad day and that I could help her by influencing her attitude. I noticed her name tag, and in a very positive tone, I said, "Hello, Tammy. How are you today?" I smiled at her the entire time and worked to get her to see me.

When she finally looked at me, she smiled and said, "Fine."

My response was, "You have a wonderful smile. Thank you for sharing it with me and brightening my day." Her smile grew, and you could instantly see her demeanor change. Such is the power of one—you can remedy someone's entire day with a simple act of kindness, and you can alter an entire environment through your attitude.

I'll never forget my first days as the new fleet master chief at the old Navy Annex in Washington, DC. I routinely walked through the building to see the many groups working various aspects of the manpower, personnel, training, and education programs and policy for our navy. As I passed others in the hallways, I noticed that everyone avoided making eye contact with anyone they would meet. I, however, like to greet everyone, and when I said good morning, they would often act as if they had not heard me. I could have just said, "OK, that's the way it is here in DC," but I refused to allow others to change me, so I worked at changing my atmosphere. I continued to say good morning and offered a smile every time.

Have you ever smiled at someone and taken notice of what occurred? Try it once, and I bet you will get a smile in return. As I continued my efforts with a smile and a greeting, the others eventually began to do the same; I soon started to notice that they were even having conversations in the hallways too. With a simple act of kindness, we (not I) increased communication across the entire team and changed our culture.

How you perceive yourself and whether you understand the impact you can have on others will affect your approach. If you approach your day with a positive mind-set and try to find the good in others rather than being critical of them, you will see the positive impact you can have. For instance, you can enable your team to contribute to creating a climate that benefits everyone. Positivity is infectious, and so is negativity. How would you change a negative into a positive? As Captain Erdossy would say, kill them with kindness.

Changing Your Attitude and Approach to Improve Your Personal and Professional Environment

I mentioned my family in the introduction and how we often discuss leadership. You see, I consider my family a team as well. Many of the ideas in this book are ones you should discuss and use at your own home. Imagine not arguing about bad behavior with your spouse or kids but rather complimenting them on the good things they are doing. Notice what occurs when you try this—I bet you will start to see that they want to please you more and seek more praise from you. Having a negative attitude will only get you negative behavior; however, having a positive attitude will get you even more positive behavior in return. Through your approach, you set the tone.

One of my favorite books to read on this thought process is *Whale Done!*, by Ken Blanchard. This book changed my life, and I encourage you to read it and then implement its ideas at home and at work. You be the judge of the outcome. I know you will soon be another advocate for spreading the word on positive leadership. If you are not a positive leader yourself, you cannot expect to be part of a positive culture. You can use the power of one insofar as you can change your own attitude and approach. Only when you address this can you expect to also change the environment in which you operate.

Sea Stories, Sailor Grams, and Never Forgetting the Basics

In chapters two through eight, I will go over the guiding principles that I established in presenting the Power of Positive Leadership. When conducting any presentation or discussion, it is necessary to ensure that you can connect with the audience. My approach has been to share my experiences in such a way that my audience understands how they shaped me into the leader that I am today. During my service in the navy, my peer group termed these stories *sea stories*. This term was passed on to us by our mentors as they shared their stories. Whether you have sea stories too or have encountered similar situations in your professional or personal life, the ability to capture these experiences and translate them into positive messages for your audience will determine your success.

The chapters following those offer additional points. During my time as a fleet master chief I worked to spread the POP Leadership message across the entire US Navy by creating documents that I titled *sailor grams*. I felt that if we were going to continue to grow as a team of leaders, we needed to continue to discuss leadership. Through my years of learning and leading, I've come to realize that when your team starts to struggle in various areas, you have to return to the basics.

A story I would often tell to make this point is about a professional baseball player. Can you imagine making millions of dollars for being successful just one third of the time? If you can hit the baseball and reach base safely at the professional level with a .300 batting average, you are a rare find. In the navy, that type of "success" is considered failure. However, when a professional baseball player starts to struggle and suddenly hits at only a .200 batting average, he returns to the basics. He may start by putting a baseball on a batting tee and swinging through it, all the while watching himself on video to ensure that he has a balanced approach. This would enable him to use the greatest amount of force and accuracy. Once he did well with this and made his corrections, he could then start to swing at a slow-pitched ball, or what some would call a soft toss. He would monitor his swing closely, make adjustments, and then pick up speed until he ultimately returned to speeds of more than ninety miles an hour. The professional baseball player understands that focusing on the basics and studying the opposing pitcher makes all the difference between success and failure.

This story illustrates that you must likewise return to the basic principles of leadership when you are struggling to lead your organization to success. You must study leadership ideas while also working to understand the team you lead. In the US Navy, failure is never an option when conducting a mission. But do failures occur? Absolutely—and when they do, a great deal of studying takes place to ultimately ensure that lessons are learned and mistakes are not repeated. I used sailor grams as an opportunity to enable other leaders to focus on the basics and discuss leadership with their teams to promote success. As you read the rest of the book, I ask you to think about how you currently foster awareness by focusing on the basics of leadership, both for others and for yourself. Remember, as you communicate effectively and succeed as a leader, so does your team.

POP Points

- Every member of your team is a leader.
- Each member has the ability to influence the atmosphere of the team and change the overall culture.
- Always kill others with kindness. You can change a person's day with one simple act.
- Your attitude and approach shape your atmosphere.
- How you perceive yourself and whether you understand the impact you can have on others will affect your approach.
- Positivity is infectious, and so is negativity!
- You have the power to change your own attitude and approach.
- Sometimes you must return to the basics of leadership.

Recommended reading: *Whale Done!*, by Ken Blanchard.

CHAPTER 2

Power of Positive (POP)

ALWAYS REMEMBER THOSE who have supported you through positive leadership and provided you mentorship on your journey to success. Bring this leadership trait forward by ensuring that those you lead are afforded the same opportunities as you were through effective communication, education, and leadership. The future success of your team depends directly on how you educate them on leadership and how you display such skills through your character. This occurs not only while you are in the workplace but 24 hours a day, 7 days a week, and 365 days a year. Those you lead will replicate what they see in you, as they watch what you say and, more importantly, what you do all the time. You are viewed as successful, and they will seek to replicate your behavior to achieve their own success. Pay your success forward through the power of your positive leadership.

Building on Foundations of Leadership Learning and Valuing Mentorship

Positive energy is something that one must experience from within. It is true that there are many factors to one's exterior that can be perceived as negative. However, only you can decide if you are going to allow those negative factors to affect you.

I have always been strong in my faith and the belief that God has a plan for me. My mom and dad instilled this in me very early in life. As I have focused my efforts on learning about leadership, I have come to realize that there are many leadership lessons in the Bible. If you are a

9

person of faith, or even if you are not, I encourage you to seek wisdom and positive energy from the Bible and other sources of inspiration. I also encourage everyone to remain focused on positive energy by reading leadership books and stories that may inspire you. Whether about life, sports, or even politics, there are stories of leadership and inspiration that you may be able to connect with. Find that positivity in your life, and then work toward maintaining that focus as you continue to learn.

An important element in any leader's success is surrounding him- or herself with other effective leaders and mentors. As we continue to focus on the basics of leadership, we must understand that mentorship is a key component of a successful team. Therefore, the most senior of leaders must exercise it so that the entire team can experience it. Reflect on your own personal success and those people who have helped you to develop into the person you are today. You will soon realize that success is never achieved alone. You have many to thank for your current success. If you asked them how you could pay them back for all that they have done for you, in almost every case, they would tell you to pay it forward. A leader recognizes that his or her actions in supporting others projects a character trait that they hope their team will replicate. Why is that? A leader knows that as he or she develops this trait in others, his or her influence also increases across the team. If a leader is constantly working to ensure effective communication and develop others into leaders, all others on the team will work toward the same goal. This will ultimately grow the strength of the entire team.

Coach Herb Brooks, Mentoring

Think back to a situation in your life in which something that seemed so difficult to achieve actually was achieved because of the leader of a team. I like to think about the movie *Miracle*, about the 1980 US Olympic hockey team. The Soviet players made for a well-trained team, and they were led by an aggressive coach whose opinion aligned with their nation's expectation that they would always be the greatest hockey team in the world. Prior to these Olympics, they were, in fact, the best of the best. However, along came the US hockey team.

The Olympic committee knew they would have to find the very best coach to achieve the success they hoped for, and they truly did find him. Coach Herb Brooks knew that if his team was going to win gold, they had to condition and prepare themselves like no one had ever done before. He studied his opponents and identified the weaknesses of the other teams while also working to identify the strengths he would need to look for when selecting his own team. Once he had put his team together, he spent endless hours on preparation, both for what he had to do as a coach and for what his players had to do. He had to project a vision to his team and effectively communicate to them why his infinite commitment and their extreme conditioning was necessary. He had to educate them on how to work as a team—to break down any barriers that existed from previous relationships—and make them understand the need to unify and focus on their mission. He had to show them that his allegiance to their success was stronger than anyone else's.

And so, he mentored them—not just as players but also as growing young men. He brought them into his home, and he showed genuine interest in their personal and professional development. He made them believe in his vision, and he made them believe that they were capable, if they worked hard and prepared well, of doing something no one else would have thought possible. The gold medal that team earned is probably one of the most recognized wins in the history of the Olympics. Because of a hockey game, the American nation came together to celebrate a previously unimaginable success.

Another leadership concept that Coach Brooks exercises is something that Joel Osteen discusses in his book *Everyday a Friday*: *have to* versus *get to*. A good friend of mine, Command Master Chief Bryan Exum, shared this with me during one of our many leadership discussions. Think of how many times a day you state that you have to do something. You say, "I have to go to work today," "I have to do the laundry," or "I have to fix dinner." You could go on and on with the different situations that you apply this to. Well, each time a hockey player or assistant coach questioned Brook's approach, he made it clear to all of them that they did not *have to* be there; indeed, they could leave whenever they wanted to. They *got to* play hockey on the US Olympic team just as you *get to* go to work, do the laundry, and fix dinner. By changing the word, you may just start to understand that many people in the world are not as fortunate as you; they can only wish they had the opportunity to do the tasks that most of us take for granted. You have to be unemployed for only a short period of time before you appreciate how special it was that you got to go to work at all, and how much you miss your job.

The players on the US Olympic hockey team were constantly reminded of this and could easily visualize the number of players who had been cut from the roster and who only wished they were still on the team. Coach Brooks had himself been cut from a previous Olympic hockey team that had gone on to win a gold medal. He knew how it felt, and so, he often reiterated that his players *got to* be on the team. They soon started to believe in his tactics for preparation. They finally knew they were part of something very special because they did not have to play hockey, but they got to. And they became a very important part of US Olympic history. Putting this into perspective now, how many things do you have to do compared to the number of things you get to do? Joel Osteen is an outstanding author, and I encourage you take some time to read his books on leadership and faith.

There are many lessons in the movie *Miracle*, and it can be used as another tool to communicate the importance of leadership. Coach Brook's approach may have been considered harsh, or as some would even say, negative. But he pushed those young men to see that they were capable of achieving more than they had ever thought they could. He showed true concern for their well-being and passed on the many lessons that he had learned from others, from his time as both a player and a coach. He was determined to pay it forward, and I am sure that those players continue to reflect on their coach and the life lessons he shared to enable them to grow into the men they are today. I believe they honor their coach by paying their own life lessons forward as they now work to lead and develop others.

Is there any doubt in your mind after watching this movie that the coach was committed to his team 24 hours a day, 7 days a week, and 365 days a year? His players—and his family—saw that he was and shared in his success. He provided everyone an approach to follow so that they too could achieve any goal they set in life. If you are not all in, you will likely not achieve your goal. If your commitment is strong and you continue to learn along the way, you will effectively educate your team while also communicating your expectations to them. As you grow as a leader, your teammates will grow as leaders, and the likelihood of success will increase as well. The power of your positive leadership will affect others as you continue to invest in them. Showing them that you must also invest in yourself as a leader will make them even stronger.

As you watch Coach Brooks nurture those young men, you will see how much they came to value the commitment not only to his work but—and maybe more importantly—to his family too. It can be difficult to balance work and family life, but having the love and support of your family can be a strong enabler. This was the case with Coach Brooks, whose wife was a leader for her family.

Mentoring and Sharing a Long Life's Journey

I have read many leadership books during my life. My first was Donald T. Phillips's *Lincoln on Leadership*, a great book for any new leader looking to start reading and learning. I have always been a fan of Abraham Lincoln, so it seemed like the best choice for me.

Cheryl and I were once on vacation in Tennessee when we stopped at the Loretta Lynn Ranch, which explores her past as a cole miner's daughter. While in one of the country stores, we were purchasing a couple jars of the jam that was made at the ranch. Cheryl noticed that the young lady behind the counter was reading a book on Abraham Lincoln.

This immediately prompted a great discussion, and the young lady mentioned her passion to read everything she could about the president. She shared a story in which a customer from a few months prior had noticed the same thing and sent books to her at the ranch. The customer had addressed them to *the young lady who loves to read Lincoln.* Everyone there knew who this was.

I told her about *Lincoln on Leadership,* and for the next ten minutes, we talked and got to know each other a little bit. She shared her dreams of going to college and why she was so inspired by President Lincoln. I shared stories of my time in the navy and how I had developed a program called POP Leadership. I also asked if she had ever read *Lincoln on Leadership.* She had not, so I told her that I would send her a copy to add to her reading list. I gave her one of my navy retirement coins and asked for her address. She hesitated, and I could appreciate this given I was a complete stranger to her and she was a young lady still in high school. However, I think our talk and Cheryl's presence made her feel more comfortable. She provided the information as she stated that she really wanted to read the book. *Katlyn Lynn* was the name given with the address, and Cheryl asked if she was of any relation to Mrs. Loretta Lynn. As it turned out, she is the woman's great-granddaughter, and she lived and worked there at the ranch.

I sent Katlyn the book as well as another I felt strongly about sharing with her. I love to share leadership books, especially with young people, as it creates an opportunity for future leadership discussions. Just as I had done with many others, I asked Katlyn to send me a note after she had finished the book to tell me what she thought of it. She was a wonderful young lady, who I could tell was going to go far in life and have a very positive impact on others. This was an unexpected experience on our trip but a very welcome one that I will forever remember. Thank you, Ms. Katlyn Lynn.

What I often find when I reach out to others is that, although I may be the one trying to spread a positive message, those whom I engage usually have a larger positive impact on me as I learn from them. Forming relationships with others in the most unexpected of places enables you to develop, as it provides you the opportunity to learn from others, from their experiences. Building on the foundations that others have given you in the past and mentoring others as you continue to learn in all aspects of your life—24 hours a day, 7 days a week, and 365 days a year—enables you to stay focused on first growing through the power of positive and then paying it forward to the benefit of those you encounter. Live, and project your journey with positive energy, and you will get twice as much out of it than you could ever give to others.

POP Points

- Those you lead will replicate what they see in you, their leader.
- Positive energy must be experienced from within.
- Successful people surround themselves with good people.
- Mentorship is a key component of a successful team.
- Successful leaders have a strong commitment to success.
- Successful leaders have great vision, and they effectively communicate that vision so that others can see they are capable of achieving it too.
- Building relationships will enable you and your team to grow.

Recommended reading: *Everyday a Friday,* by Joel Olstean, and *Lincoln on Leadership,* by Donald T. Phillips.

CHAPTER 3

Passion with Compassion

EXERCISE POSITIVE LEADERSHIP by showing your team how they are valued. In the military, you do not often get to select the team who will be assigned to you for completing any given mission. They are sent to you based on a need for a specific skill set that will contribute to the mission's success. Every position would not have been created unless it was a necessity, so there is great value in having every single member on your team. The same is true in any corporation as a position would not have been created had the leader or human resource department not needed it. In that situation, you would have greater say in the person you were hiring because of your ability to evaluate and place a new team member. In both cases, every person is needed to provide some function and should therefore be shown that they are a valuable member of your team.

Value and Connect with All Leaders

On a ship at sea, the most junior member of the crew may be working as a food service attendant in the crew galley scullery, scrubbing pots and pans. It is not a job that requires a great deal of skill, but without someone performing this function, no meal would ever be prepared—which would result in a very unhappy crew. In a fundamental way, the young sailor in the scullery may be the most important member of the team.

Sanitation in the galley is extremely important to ensure the health and overall welfare of the crew. Those of us who have served at sea understand that a good wholesome meal has a significant impact on our morale. Although the most important role of the ship may be to provide an option for our nation's security around the world, the primary function of each team member is a necessary link in the chain. Therefore, every member of the team must be made to know their value. It is up to you, as their leader, to declare how instrumental they are to the success of the mission.

Only weeks before my dad passed away, he shared a book with me that he had obviously spent a great deal of time reviewing throughout his life. It was *The Purpose Driven Life,* by Rick Warren. This book based on Christian spirituality has a very clear message: for one to be happy in life, one must experience a sense of purpose and accomplishment.

As a leader, you are also, in many ways, a cheerleader for your team. You must keep them motivated and focused on achieving your goals and those of the organization you serve. Showing that you value them can be done by following President Abraham Lincoln's lead. He needed to be out among his people to understand their challenges, and doing so revealed how much he cared about them and valued their perspectives. Of course, he had to be able to relate to people at all levels of society, and he had to relay that their work was contributing to making the nation better for everyone. Even those who are considered the lowest leaders in your organization will feel they play an important part if you show them not only how their efforts are valued but that their good work translates into success for the entire team too.

Positive Reinforcement

Always display a passion for what you do as a leader through your actions. If you are a leader, your team members will always be watching you, and they will thereby learn the traits of positive leadership. When Abraham Lincoln led in the Oval Office, he understood that his generals, leading the fight in the Civil War, did not belong in an office in Washington, DC. He knew they had to be out with their men, leading by example. If you expect positive results from your team, you must provide them positive leadership and support them in accomplishing the task at hand. Rarely in history have the dictatorships of powerful armed leaders succeeded for very long. Fear and mistreatment do not motivate people to support you; they motivate people to work against you in the hopes that a better option will turn up. I often use the behavior of my dogs as an example. When I tell my dog to sit and he understands the command and sits down, I give him a treat. Why? Because he then believes that he will receive a treat whenever he follows my command to complete the task. However, if I told him to sit and he failed to do so and I started to beat him, he would be more likely to fight back and maybe even bite me as he would not like the treatment.

As I mentioned earlier, one of my favorite books on positive leadership is Ken Blanchard's *Whale Done!*, which shows a leader who is struggling in his relationships both at work and at home. It demonstrates how the positive reinforcement of a desired behavior enables the trainers at Sea World to train what are considered some of the most dangerous mammals on the face of the earth to do tricks for an audience. Instead of being critical of others, he looks inward and modifies his own behavior, and this immediately starts to change the way in which others respond to him. Make this book a priority if you have not already read it.

You get from others what you give to them. As you give them positive reinforcement and see the good in doing so, they will sense your passion for what you do. They will see your success and work hard to replicate it for themselves. Therefore, you will foster a positive change much faster than you would fighting any negativity within your team.

Developing a Vision of Success

Develop in your team today what they will need in the future for continued success. Leaders at all levels should work to become visionaries. They must see beyond their current task or the service they are providing. Whether you work in the corporate world or in the military, being prepared for the future, and preparing those you lead to meet future demands, will determine your success. Essential to meeting these demands is the ability to plan and then execute. Your team will experience many benefits when this is accomplished correctly. A key element can be ensuring that they are involved in developing the vision and then having them help you with any planning. When you communicate properly, you will be able to show them how valuable they are to the team. If you expect them to be successful in the task at hand, you must first give them a sense of responsibility. However, follow-up is also necessary.

As you lead in this manner, those same efforts will be replicated at all levels of leadership, and you will find that the effectiveness of your organization has grown so that it can accomplish a great deal more. The team's competitive spirit will similarly grow, and you will find that every member is creating more ideas for the present and future development of them all. Remember, the strength of the entire team is greater than the strength of any one. If you want others to see you as a leader, you must first inspire them to follow and then guide them to success. Once they achieve that success, you must give them the credit they deserve. Leaders do not need credit; they need results from those they lead.

Leading with Passion and Teaching Compassion

I experienced a situation like this when I first started my new position as the command master chief of USS *George Washington*. In any navy organization, you have teams of leaders at various levels. On a navy ship, you have a wardroom that consists of the commissioned officers, a chief petty officer mess that includes all the senior enlisted leaders in pay grades E-7 through E-9, and a first class petty officer mess that includes all those in E-6. Those who belong to the wardroom and the chief petty officer mess are automatically considered members of the group. The first class petty officer mess can be a voluntary organized group of which first class petty officers can become a member. When I arrived to the ship, only 30 of the 350 first class petty officers on board were members. This bothered me, as it showed a separation in a leadership group that I found detrimental to leading our sailors. Displaying any separation among leaders will only lead to poor results. Our sailors needed to see unified leadership at all levels, so I brought all 350 first class petty officers together, along with their department chief petty officers, and announced my expectations of all first class petty officers. First and foremost, I wanted them to know how much I valued their leadership of our sailors and that their unity would enable the greatest opportunity for success.

The first class mess is supposed to be a learning environment where we teach our first-class petty officers how to become chiefs. If our sailors did not want to be a part of that group, then I assumed that they did not want to be a chief petty officer. In the performance evaluation process, their performance was compared to that of their peers and given a ranking. In the ship's history, and due to the large number of first class petty officers, this had only ever been conducted at the department level in small groups. I had felt this practice needed to change to reinforce the importance of the first class petty officers' leadership role. So, with the support of Captain Martin Erdossy III, myself and the department leading chiefs had taken on ranking all 350 first class petty officers, and we shared our findings with the department heads for their review and concurrence.

The command master chief and the command leadership team would now have a say, across the entire command, in what was important to leading at this level. The department head leaders all bought into this idea once I presented it to them, since it would afford those who could not be promoted for years the opportunity to be ranked against others throughout the ship. Some departments had only one first class petty officer, and that first class petty officer's performance was never adequately compared to others. Being ranked number one of one meant very little to a selection board, but being ranked number twenty-five of more than three hundred could, and ultimately did, make a difference.

In my closing comments to the first class petty officers, I expressed to them that I needed their unity and support. I challenged them to come up with ways that they could make the command more efficient and their sailors stronger. I would meet with and mentor them personally, over the course of my tour, and invest in them if they would only invest in the sailors. Needless to say, those first class petty officers responded. Within a month, they had well over three hundred as active members of the first class petty officer mess. They worked to get involved in the warfare qualifications of all sailors. As a result, our damage control skills grew significantly, and over the course of our deployment, we had the most qualifications in the ship's history. Our sailors were smarter, they were invested in securing success, and they were taking their leadership role seriously, at every level of command. They were well-behaved not only at sea but also during port visits. They were dedicated, and they did not want to lose what they had worked so hard for.

Toward the end of the deployment, I invited all the first class petty officers to the chief petty officer mess for an ice cream social to thank them. In the past, it had been rare for anyone other than a chief petty officer to enter that mess. Ours agreed that we needed to do something special to show the first class petty officers our appreciation, and it was a great event. We also used ice cream socials to break down other barriers, but I will share more on that with you later. The ranking process had involved all the department leading chief petty officers and taken seven ten-hour days. Fortunately, it proved to be successful, as we advanced more first class petty officers to chief petty officer that year than any prior. Some who had been deserving but could never break free from their pack were finally promoted after they had been compared to the whole group. I am grateful to everyone who responded and inspired success for all. It took having a vision, being able to communicate it effectively, gaining support at all levels, and then all of us carrying out our mission together. It was the work of those first class petty officers that really made our entire team stronger and enabled us to grow. I will forever remember them for their inspiring resolve. Thank you, shipmates—you know who you are.

Having Compassion and Ensuring Team Success

Show compassion when a team member needs assistance; this is when they need your leadership the most. How you support those in need during the hard times will determine the level of trust and loyalty that develops within your team. Also, always be mindful that as you deal with the misfortune of one person, others are watching to see how you react, in the case they may one day make a similar mistake.

Invest time with your team to learn their needs and you will develop trust and confidence, through your actions, that will enable them to reach out to you when they need assistance. This is an important statement. If you desire your team to support your goals and reflect your values, as their leader, you need to spend time with them often and communicate with them effectively. Moreover, you need to show them that you are willing to invest in them, to develop their capabilities and contribution to the team. If you want them to have a strong commitment to you, then you must have a strong commitment to them. Always remember that you get what you give.

I have many stories from my time aboard USS *George Washington*. The aircraft carrier is a huge organization. As the command master chief, I led over two hundred chief petty officers who in turn led a crew of over three thousand sailors. As leader of the chief petty officer mess, I knew I needed to invest in this group. This became my primary focus as I reported to the carrier. I knew that the coming together of this team would make a difference in the level of success we achieved.

There were seventeen departments aboard, each of which had a leading chief petty officer. This was my core group of leaders, who I greatly depended upon to keep me on course. I met with this group at least once a week to ensure that we were working together and toward meeting our command goals. I encouraged them to tell me when they felt I was off course. I needed their honest feedback, and I realized that as their leader, I also served them and their sailors. In getting support, I grasped that I, first and foremost, needed to give support. As a group, we agreed to create a training committee for the entire chief petty officer's mess, and we conducted training twice a month. This training focused on leadership development and program knowledge, so that we could increase general awareness about the missions we were focusing on at the time. Every session was followed by a meeting so that I could share and gain areas of concern that required our group's support. As always, I encouraged them to provide honest feedback on how to accomplish a number of things. I may have been their leader, but I knew that all their minds combined were far greater than my single mind. In doing this, I also enabled them to take responsibility for the various tasks and our overall success.

Everyone needs the opportunity to lead, and when anyone presents a great idea, that person needs to take on the responsibility of seeing it through to the end. And he or she will be the most passionate about enabling the success of all involved. My approach brought my team together and developed their trust in one another. At the same time, it gave me more time to focus on other things. However, I never lost focus on their tasks, as they would report to me and I would direct them, removing barriers as necessary. Leadership is less about doing things yourself and more about preparing your team members to lead so that you can maximize their success.

Supporting and Producing Leaders

We once had a command managed equal opportunity leader assigned to the ship. When I reported for duty, I had a meeting with her, as I did with all major program leaders. She was a great educator, but little was being done to utilize her skills. She was also poorly received by many of the department leaders, as they saw her only as someone who brought them complaints from the people working in their departments. We needed to change that perception of her. And so, we laid out a plan in which I would visibly support the program she led, because it was extremely important. We also developed a prevention plan that would improve the way she communicated with the department leaders. Instead of focusing only on complaints, she would utilize her amazing speaking and teaching skills.

We thus reduced the number of complaints and even encouraged the resolution of minor issues at the lowest possible level. At the same time, we raised morale, as our sailors could see that we were prioritizing the programs that enabled their success. She routinely met with department leaders to give them updates on what she was seeing and offered them education plans to overcome any shortfalls. As soon as she showed that she was there to enable their success, they completely reversed their perception of her—another instance of getting what you give. Needless to say, this one woman inspired our entire command to succeed, and she was promoted accordingly.

Senior Chief Treste Loving remains a very good friend of mine today, and she continues to have a positive impact on equal employment opportunities and diversity development in the civilian sector. Such stories display how investing in others, as part of a group or as an individual, determines the level of success your team can achieve. If you invest in your team, they will invest in you. Have compassion when a teammate may be struggling, and be willing to help them all. Your commitment to your team will grant you the strongest of commitments in return. Effect loyalty and professionalism at all times. Your team members are always watching, and your character—in and outside of the workplace—will determine how much they feel they can trust you as a leader.

Having Compassion for Those You Lead When They Need It the Most

There is an old saying in the military that we work hard, and I can assure you that our service members really do work hard, but we play hard too. In the navy of many years ago, this mentality triggered the visual of a drunken, cursing sailor. I can also assure you that our professional sailors and all other service members are a far cry from this today. In fact, we have very high expectations for personal and professional conduct.

However, junior personnel will replicate the behavior of their leaders, and they may just lose their trust in you if your own conduct does not measure up. This is the case for any leader, in or out of the military. You cannot expect something of others and then expect less of yourself.

Another critical factor in knowing those you lead is being able to identify when they may be struggling with something at work or at home that is causing stress or even depression. In a military environment, we take this very seriously due to the highly stressful situations, the time away from home, and often the actions we must carry out in defense of our nation. When someone is depressed, you will immediately notice a change in their attitude, which will potentially impact their ability to perform. You may see a reduction in production, or poor decision-making, that can affect not only that one person but your entire team as well. Of course, your immediate concern will be for the individual. However, depending on the number of people they are leading, this situation can have a significant impact on the organization at large. As previously mentioned, positivity is infectious, but so is negativity—even when an individual cannot appreciate what he or she is doing.

As leaders, we always want to fix things so that our efforts can continue and improve. Having a conversation with the stressed or depressed person will show him or her that you care. This display of concern is important; however, it is also important to understand that you may not be able to help this person relieve some of the stress, or you may not be able to help this person deal with the depression. The affected person needs to ask for help, and—more importantly—you need to help this person identify that he or she might be dealing with depression. It is essential that you support this person, but direct him or her to get counseling on how to address or cope with the depression. In some situations, a doctor may even need to prescribe him or her a medication. Unless you are a trained professional, you should simply offer resources so that this person can seek the necessary assistance.

Over the past ten years, our military has grown a great deal in this area. It now recognizes that depression is not a weakness and that we must have resources in place to help any service member who may be dealing with it so that we can retain them as an integral part of our team. Attrition in the workforce is a concern of both the military and the civilian sector, as it has the potential to set progress back. Never forget that your people are your most important resource. As you work to support those who are struggling, your unaffected team members will be watching to see how you handle the situation. Stress and depression can affect anyone. If others see that you are not actually supporting someone who needs help, and that you would rather just dismiss that person, they will ask themselves, "What if this were me? Would I have to worry about my job?" Obviously, this can have a significantly negative impact on your environment.

As the leader, you set the tone. You must have the passion to be a great leader, and you must commit yourself to your goals and the vision you communicate to others. But first you must understand the need to show compassion for those you lead, as you will not complete the mission without the help of your team. Passion with compassion is a concept that all leaders must exercise to profit from the power of positive leadership.

POP Points

- Show your team that they are valued.
- Be out among your team members so that you can understand their challenges and show them that you value their perspectives.
- Emphasize the importance of those leaders at the lowest levels and how their efforts translate to success for the entire team.
- Always display a passion for what you do and educate others through your positive leadership traits.
- Develop in your team today what they will need in the future for continued success.
- Have a vision, communicate it effectively, obtain support at all levels, and then guarantee that everyone works together toward success.
- Show compassion when a team member is in need of assistance. This is when they need their leader the most.
- If you want your team to have a strong commitment to you, you must have a strong commitment to them.
- Invest in your team and they will invest in you.
- Exercise loyalty and professionalism at all times, in and out of the workplace.
- You cannot expect something of others and then expect less of yourself.
- Never forget that your people are your most important resource!

Recommended reading: *The Purpose Driven Life*, by Rick Warren.

CHAPTER 4

❦

Pride Projection

PRIDE PROJECTION IS a simple concept. But what does this mean to you as a leader? Take a moment to truly think about what pride projection means to you. Some of you may see it as a way in which you carry yourself, and I would tend to agree with you. Carrying yourself with pride in front of those you lead is not arrogance; nor does it imply that you are proud of your team due to your leadership alone. Pride projection is defined as showing your team that you have respect for yourself, which enables you to have respect for others. You demonstrate that you understand all people are incapable of knowing everything. You have the self-confidence and self-respect to know that you can and should continue to develop. You respect your people enough to show them that you can learn from their experience—that you are proud to depend on them for their expertise in promoting the entire team. They will know by your behavior that you know not all the world needs to revolve around your decisions. Remember that your people will watch you based on your past level of success. They want to learn from your experience too, and they want to understand how to better communicate with you.

Reading Is Fundamental

How do you get your team to understand your thought process through means other than just your verbal communications? I would say to you that, as a leader, you must continue your learning. A great way to show them that you are doing this is by reading leadership books. When you meet with your teams, carry your current book with you. I assure you it will spark their curiosity. They will see that you are seeking knowledge, and this may even incite a leadership discussion. Ultimately, your intent is that they get the book for themselves and start reading and learning too.

If you would like those you lead to better support you, they need to get to know you so that they connect with you. What better way to do so than for them to start reading a book that you are reading and then have a conversation with you about a concept that may apply to the work you are doing. It is one thing to hear an idea from you, their leader, but if they can study and learn from the experiences of others, they may just exceed your expectations. Consider starting a book club on leadership books. Give them an hour each day for reading and discussion. Adults learn best through interaction. If you show them that you value leadership development, and you give them the time to learn while on the clock, they will see that you appreciate their personal and professional growth.

Visible Positive Impacts

Those you lead are evaluating your professionalism and overall character twenty-four hours a day. Never forget your team members' desire to achieve your level of success, or that they want to be like you. During my POP presentations, I talk about how this lesson came to me after visiting with my mom and dad. At the time, my dad was using a walker, and as I watched him walk across the floor, I noted that his right foot was angled outward at about forty-five degrees—and that this is the same way I walk. I did not think much of it until I returned home and Anthony entered the house. I saw him walking the same way, so I asked him, "Why does your foot turn out that way?"

His response was, "I don't know. I have always done it that way."

A couple hours later, Jason came home. And guess what—he was walking the same way! I asked him why and, of course, I received the same response. I then asked him, "Can you walk with your foot straight?"

He tried, and he said, "Well, I guess I can."

All of us are capable of walking with our foot straight, but none of us do. I am willing to bet that if I could see my grandfather walk, he would also walk the same. My point is that we all subconsciously do what we observe in others. As a leader, you must set a visible positive example even more than you must use positive words.

Visible Impacts You Often Do Not See until It Is Too Late

How many times have you heard that a positive outlook will help you to overcome an illness or at least give you a greater opportunity of recovery? Those who deal with terminal illnesses are often the most inspirational to others. In many cases, they understand that their lives are shorter than most and that they must find a way to use the time they do have in a positive manner.

In 2007, I learned that my dad had been diagnosed with cancer. At the time, it appeared that the cancer was in his stomach and that it could be treated. I think he shielded us from the truth so that we wouldn't worry, but ultimately, he ended up with pancreatic cancer. His doctors performed a Whipple procedure to remove the tumor. He then suffered through chemotherapy and radiation treatment. Dad said the doctors were optimistic about his chances of recovery. As anyone would do if a parent was being treated for cancer, I was trying to be optimistic too while at the same time doing research on pancreatic cancer and learning the real statistics of this lethal disease.

My dad's illness coincided with the start of my development of POP Leadership. Dad had worked for Marriot for many years as well as for some other organizations, including the State of Pennsylvania. One of the places he had worked that I had always enjoyed was Farrell's Ice Cream Parlor. He had led the expansion of this fabulous business across the country until the day Marriot had decided to leave the restaurant industry. He had always been a manager in his business life, and—maybe even more importantly—he was forever a leader in his family and personal life. Deep in his faith, he believed in providing service to others, and I can remember times when he led in youth sporting associations. I can also recall a memorable time when we lived in Greene County, Virginia, and Dad led efforts to establish the first Catholic Church in the county.

He traveled often in those days, so my mom would end up handling most of the discipline issues. When she called Dad in to help, my siblings and I all knew we were in for big trouble and a stern hand. Times were different then; the occasional spanking was given out, but they were rare, as you could tell that they hurt Mom and Dad more than us. Both parents had a lot of patience from raising six kids, and they worked hard to give us as much as they could and always ensure that we had the things we needed to be successful in life. I am proud to look at our family today and see that all six kids are successful in their own ways and doing very well in life. We have our parents, Lester and Kathleen Benning, to thank for this, and for the foundation they provided us.

As Dad was going through his treatment in Pennsylvania, I was serving in Virginia. I felt maybe POP could help him the same way it was helping me. Most importantly, I felt that sharing it with him could create a stronger bond between us and enable us to have leadership conversations. My dad did not like talking on the phone much, and I did not always find it easy to talk with him. But this did offer us the opportunity to learn from each other, and I hope it helped him to overcoming the cancer.

As I was developing POP, I sent pages of information to my dad for his feedback. I had others helping me as well, but having my dad's perspective would hopefully provide me a perspective of my dad that I had not considered before. Although we did not have many leadership discussions throughout our life together, I did learn from his example. I often wish I had been more engaging with him and sought out his advice more. We live and learn in life, and because of my shortcomings in this relationship with my dad, I now work to ensure that I discuss leadership with my two boys and share my experiences with them so that we can all learn together. Doing this has enabled us to develop a very strong friendship that I wish I could have had with my dad. Asking for his advice did help us to talk more, and I always appreciated his feedback. It brought us closer together.

Sadly, our time with him was short. We brought everyone together as my dad wanted us to celebrate my mom's seventieth birthday as a family. I think we knew that he wanted to see us all together one last time. During that visit, Dad found a way to spend some time with each of us. He shared a few items from his US Marine Corps uniform that he obviously cherished. I now cherish them, and they will be passed down to my sons. I did not know much about Dad's service, but I did know the saying *once a marine, always a marine.* I asked him if I could have one of the black ties in his closet. From that time on, I wore that tie with my service dress blue uniform to honor my dad. He also showed me the degrees in religious studies that he had worked hard to complete in the last year of his life and which I knew nothing about. He wanted to show his children, in his own way, his connection to and appreciation for all of us. My dad knew that he was dying, and he showed us the importance of living every day as if you are dying. My youngest brother Mike gave one of the eulogies at Dad's service and used the expression *whatever it takes.* That applied to our dad and our mom as they both did whatever it took to care for their family and provide a good example for us.

I will never forget the last time my dad said good-bye. It is the only time I can remember him saying these three words to me: he placed his hands on both sides of my face and kissed me on the lips and said, "I love you, boy." I do not recall him ever sharing emotion like that before, and I felt it must have taken a great amount of courage for him to do it then. I knew he loved me, but never in my life had I known it more than I did at that moment. My two boys and I departed the hospital and headed back to Virginia, and a few days later, Dad left us. I think my sisters and brothers were somewhat upset that I was not there for him when he passed away. But I think my dad had known that I would not be, so he had said his good-bye to me earlier. I am like my dad in many ways, and death is not something I handle well. I will forever remember the last moment with my dad as one full of love. It is strange that we did not talk much during his life, but now I talk to my dad every day through my prayers and thank him for the example he set for me. Thank you, Dad. I love you.

I learned from my Uncle Len, at my dad's memorial service, just how proud my dad had been of my service in the navy. I had never really heard that from Dad, but hearing it from his brother meant the world to me. This was another lesson in life, as I ensure that my sons always know how proud I am of them, and I always tell them *I love you* whenever we say good-bye. I make sure they know how much they mean to me.

After I retired from the navy in 2013, Cheryl and I drove across country. Ultimately, the trip was to see our son, Jason, who was serving in San Diego. It was also a great opportunity for us to see the country we had served for thirty years. While in San Diego, we found that Farrell's Ice Cream Parlor was making a comeback in California. We had lunch at one of the locations, and I could strongly feel my dad's presence within me. They are doing a wonderful job bringing Bob Farrell's vision back to life, as the business is now just as it was years ago. I asked to speak with the manager, and we had an enjoyable discussion about my dad. As a kid, I had thought the ice cream sundaes there were amazing. The zoo was a huge ice cream sundae that fed about twenty people and was still run around the restaurant on a stretcher to present to the birthday child at his or her party. But I had also always thought that the green river soda was exceptional, and I shared this with the manager. He made sure I had one before we ended our meal and I communicated to Cheryl what it meant to be there, at Farrell's, while I drank my green river soda.

People will depart your life in various ways. But those who truly have an impact leave you with a lasting impression, filled with loving memories, and this can never be taken from you. Many of those memories are of positive experiences that develop you into the person and leader you hoped to become. Reflecting on these experiences often, and sharing them with others, can have a very lasting and positive impact on everyone. It also enables you to honor those in the stories, remembering them as if they were alive and well. My dad is alive and well within me, and I am grateful that he can never be taken from me.

The pride you feel inside often develops because of those who are part of your life or those who have helped you to progress in life. My family, first and foremost, enable my pride to shine through. It started with two loving parents, and it grows stronger each day because of the life I share with Cheryl, our two amazing boys, and their families. This pride has also developed because of the many with whom I have served in the navy. Many of my leaders and peers, along with those whom I have served and developed, have enabled me to grow through the sharing of life and learning experiences.

Visuals make for powerful tools. Taking notice of those around you and understanding the impact they have on your life will help you to realize how important it is to project pride as well as the Power of Positive Leadership. If you are not reflecting on this, now is the time to start thinking about how you can pay POP Leadership forward through your own pride projection.

It is my hope that I have made a positive impact on others' lives, enabling them to develop. Life is a learning journey, and it is beneficial for you to share the learning experience with the many who enter your life. They may depart your life in various ways, but if you have shared a positive experience, the memory of it will forever be imbedded in your life and remain a part of you. You have the opportunity to pass this lesson on to others, to ensure that their leadership legacy continues to progress. How will you remember those along the way, and how will those you meet remember you?

POP Points

- Pride projection is about showing your team that you have a level of respect for yourself that enables you to respect others.
- As a leader, you must continue to learn. Reading leadership books can be of great value to learning new ideas.
- Your peers and subordinates are evaluating your professionalism and overall character twenty-four hours a day.
- Visuals are powerful tools—as a leader, you must be visibly positive.
- Live every day as if it is your last.
- Understand that the pride you feel inside often develops because of those closest to you. Make sure to always show your appreciation for their contributions.
- Life is a learning journey, and it benefits you to share your experiences with others.

CHAPTER 5

Empowerment: Replicating Your Leadership

YOUR TEAM WILL always seek the approval of you as their leader. It is important to provide each team member with the opportunity to lead. As you show your confidence in them, you will develop a very valuable tool: future leaders.

The Ability to Adapt and Overcome, and Replicating This in Others

Think about it—there are few, if any, in life who achieve any kind of success on their own. As you evaluate your own level of success, think about those who helped you along the way. What did they see in you, and how did they show their confidence in your abilities? Life is a learning journey with both good and bad experiences. You can control some of these experiences, but others are completely out of your hands and end up completely changing the course you thought you wanted to pursue.

Oftentimes it is not about the obstacle that life has given you but how you choose to overcome that obstacle—how you learn from it and then use it as motivation to make yourself a better person. And, maybe even more importantly, it is about how you use the experience to make those around you stronger. Life is all about opportunity, and it is often difficult to see opportunity when you are facing adversity. However, if you consider that you are not the only person in the world going through a challenging time, you may realize that you are never alone. It may only seem that you are the only one with problems.

Reach out for help when you need it, minimize the mistakes you make, and stay focused on your goals. This can make you a strong leader as well as an example for others to replicate. Live, learn, and lead. And do not be afraid to be vulnerable; allow others to see that you, too, are human and make mistakes. Help them to learn from your mistakes so that they do not make the same ones. Talk openly about how you, as their leader, hope to make them more successful. They may just be willing to help you foster success for yourself as well as others.

Once they get to know you personally, you may be surprised to find that others are willing to follow you and help you to achieve success. In turn, you will be able to help them achieve success and develop into fine leaders. You need to focus on how you can use this influence to grow together, as a team, while you also invest in your team members so that they can replicate your level of success. When they understand that you are developing their confidence, they will demonstrate professionalism and their loyalty for you. Trust and confidence are thus fostered on both sides. As your team members grow in their leadership ability and find success, you must be able to express to them that they have helped you grow as a leader too.

Listening Is the Most Important Communication Tool

Young people today are amazing, and I enjoy listening to them. As I travel the country in my current position, our team meets often with our young leaders. Why do we do this? Because we value their insight and want to learn about the challenges they face and how they feel those challenges are best dealt with. We do not have all the answers on how to fix social issues at their level or in their environment. We must therefore lean on them, and learn from them how we can ensure that our messages are not only being communicated but, more importantly, being understood. In my view, the youth in our nation are our customers, and as in the business world, we must listen to our customers.

If you are going to be successful as a leader, you absolutely must listen to those you lead. If they do not understand the message or mission you are communicating, then your efforts to lead them to success may fail. Ensure that your communications include listening and this will in turn ensure that your team understands your expectations and are pursuing the right goals. If they are not on the same page as you, then you may be spending a great deal of your time and resources chasing the wrong outcome. Does your customer want a shopping experience in which they buy products from machines, or do they desire a social experience, with other people? Look at any successful company and make your own assessment. The people make all the difference.

Be the Leader You Want Them to Replicate

Never forget that they are watching you. Be the leader you desire them to be for the future of your team.

The entire family went to IHOP when Cheryl and I were visiting our kids in Virginia Beach. Our grandson Cole was turning two. He loves his mom and dad, as you would expect, and we all love Cole. After we had finished eating, our daughter-in-law, Darcie, pulled out a container of wipes and started wiping her hands. Cole was watching her closely and reached for one of the wipes. He started to wipe his hands in the same way. Darcie then started wiping her mouth with her wipe, and Cole started to do the same with his, in the same motion. Darcie then stuck out her tongue and wiped it, just to see if Cole would also, and, of course, he did. I said to her, "Now, that is a sure sign that he is watching everything you do, so you will want to be careful with how you act, as you will eventually get the same behavior you exhibit for him." This is another way of showing that people work to replicate what they see in their leaders. Are you satisfied that you are the type of leader you want your team members to replicate?

Now, I do not recommend that you get some wipes out and wipe your tongue in front of your team just to see if they will follow your lead. But when something is not going as you think it should, I encourage you to first look at how you are leading to see if you are contributing to the problem. Always analyze yourself before you assume that the problem has been created by others. You will improve your team only if you are first working to improve yourself, and self-evaluation must be a part of your plan. Just as your kids will represent your family when they become adults, those you lead professionally will represent your team. Make sure that, just as your kids get the best of you as a parent, those you lead get the best of you as their leader.

Leadership Legacy

There have been many books written about leadership legacy. This is an important factor for any leader to consider. With good reason, the military takes it very seriously. All leaders realize that their impact in the service is limited by a specific amount of time, so it is imperative that we do our very best within that time frame. At some point, we all depart at the end of an enlistment or retire. We have the passion to ensure that the leadership torch is passed on so that the success of our nation only ever grows. We take every opportunity to make sure that our presence is not missed and that our legacy lives on in the success of our team members.

We must ask ourselves, every day we lead and no matter the situation, how we want our teams to lead after we have moved on. We understand that they are watching us. They see our success, and they hope to replicate our actions. We must therefore ensure that every leadership opportunity is a teaching moment. How would you expect those who work for you, your peers, and those you work for to deal with certain situations? Are you setting a good example for them?

Your leadership legacy is about how those who you have mentored and trained perform after you have moved on. Recognizing this while you are in the leadership position is very important. During your career, you may leave a position or, as in the military, transfer to a new billet. Part of your legacy is leaving behind a strong, functioning, and successful team, which is demonstrated when that team continues to be successful in your absence. This is the true measure of a great leader. If the opposite occurs, and the team you led and left behind fails, you must appraise your leadership skills and adjust them as necessary. At times in my career, I looked back and deliberated whether, had I done a better job, my team would not have struggled without me. This drove me to take a critical look at myself and improve for my future positions. This leads back to looking at yourself first instead of immediately assuming that the others are failures. The fact may be that our team members are failing only because we have set them up to do so.

What will your leadership legacy look like? How successful was the team you led after you left them? If you are critical of those you mentored for not maintaining some level of success, maybe you need to go look in the mirror—just saying. You have the opportunity to beget success for others, including those on your team. Teach them well, and then let them lead. Empower them, and then watch them develop and reach new levels. Empowering them will not be easy, as you will all have to develop a great deal of trust with one another. But if you give them the knowledge and the resources to grow, then one day, you just may have a magnificent legacy—one that is as empowering for you as it was for your team members.

POP Points

- Provide each team member the opportunity to lead.
- Seek help when necessary; this is not a weakness, but a strength.
- Live, learn, lead. And do not be afraid to allow others to learn from your mistakes.
- Trust and confidence are developed on both sides of a relationship.
- To be a successful leader, you must listen to those you lead.
- Be the leader you desire them to be for the future of your team.
- When issues arise, first look to yourself to ensure that you are not contributing to the problem.
- Every leadership opportunity should be a teaching moment.
- Your legacy lives on in those you have developed, mentored, and trained.

CHAPTER 6

Projecting a Positive Attitude

WE ALL HAVE difficult days in life. Whether they are associated with work or our personal lives, they all have an effect on how we carry ourselves and the way we act toward ourselves and others. First and foremost, you must be willing to take a look at yourself to know how you are acting during these difficult periods of time. Then ask yourself, "Is this how I want others to see me?"

Understanding the Impacts of Having a Bad Day

Have you ever had a boss or a coworker who, when having a bad day, would turn it into a bad day for everyone else too? Such a person is likely reaching out for someone to talk to—or struggling to the point that they just cannot see how they are treating themselves and others. This may be a good opportunity to connect or establish a stronger relationship with them to see if they need your help.

I have often shared this analogy of a leader having a bad day to further make this point. Imagine a leader in an electrical field having a bad day and arriving to his morning meeting to distribute the daily tasks. This leader just met with his team leaders and did not agree with them on the need to perform a specific task. He could not convince his leaders that the task was unnecessary. When the leader had arrived at the morning production meeting with his subordinates, he was aggravated. He then communicated to the repair team that he did not agree with the task at hand, but he had been told that it must be accomplished as directed. In his aggravated state, he had given the task to an unqualified electrician. As the electrician had tried to tell him he was not qualified, the leader had responded in anger and told the worker to just get it done. Thus, the leader lost the respect of his team, and the worker was electrocuted only to die later that day. Is this possible? Does this happen? Absolutely—and because of one very bad situation, many team members may learn a terrible life lesson that will affect them for the rest of their lives.

Changing Your Delivery

Imagine that this leader had not become so upset about the task. Imagine that he had instead accepted responsibility for the task. He would have approached the team with a more positive attitude. Had a member of the team identified that the task was unnecessary, instead of trying to accept the negative comments, the leader could have turned the task into a training opportunity for the worker who was not qualified to do it. He would have been engaged in the task to observe the learning and even had others on the team work to educate and prepare the un-qualified worker so that he could improve to a qualified level. The task would have been completed. Everyone would have gone home safely at the end of the day, and they all would have felt they had contributed to the strengthening of their team. Attitude made all the difference. And so, even on bad days, it is important to understand the impact of your attitude when it is being projected to those you lead.

How Are You Projecting Positivity?

As we learn to recognize the effects of our own negative attitude, we will be able to more easily recognize this within others. This will enable us to recognize when others need our assistance in the resolution of an issue and whether it can be dealt with in a manner that will not have a negative impact on the entire team. No matter what level of leadership you operate in, at work or at home, you have an opportunity to influence others. Would you want to be influenced by a seemingly negative person? Yes, this is another self-evaluation. It is an important part of your development. You must be able to recognize your weaknesses so that you can strengthen your capacity to have a positive impact on others. When you wake up in the morning, how do you react? Do you wake up thinking, *I am going to have a great day today*? If not, you should. You must first see yourself as a proud person who wants to enable others to learn and grow from their experiences with you. Only then will you better your ability to lead. If you wake up and say, "Oh, no—another rotten day at work," what kind of day do you think you are going to have? Only one person controls your internal pride meter. And that person is you.

If you need to strengthen yourself in any area, identify what that area is and work on it. Seek out others, such as friends or mentors, who you can confide in about how you plan to overcome the limitations that are holding you back. Let others help you; it is not a weakness to ask for help but a strength. To foster success in those you lead at work or at home, you must first set a positive example for them. Then, when it is necessary to discuss their need to improve in a certain area, they will respect your perspective a great deal more. Can you imagine someone negative in your life coming to you and telling you how you need to improve? How well would you accept their advice?

Staying Fit to Stay Positive

During my time on active duty, there was always an emphasis on the triad of maintaining a healthy lifestyle. The triad includes a healthy mind, body, and spirit. It is an important practice to be able to maintain one's overall fitness in the demanding military environment as well as in the corporate world. As the demands on us grow, we tend to start forgetting to take care of ourselves. We forget the maintenance necessary to sustain our overall health.

Your body is no different than your car. You need to routinely complete maintenance to keep it running properly. These days, cars have memory chips that must be updated to keep the various electronic systems running, such as your GPS. Your mind is no different. If you fail to keep your mind working and up to date, you are going to stop running altogether. The simplest acts, such as reading a book, can keep your mind energized. In your work life, if you stop learning, you will become outdated and worthless to the tasks that need to be done.

There are many times your mind can start to feel overwhelmed. This is probably a good indication that your mind is being overworked. Exercise, even a small amount, will assist in relieving stress. The mind can also struggle when you are feeling tired, and you can start to develop aches and pains as a result of not exercising. Take the time to create a physical regiment. It does not need to be a trip to the gym three times a week. It can be something as simple as a ten-minute walk three times a week. Part of the mental relief from exercise is the knowledge that you are doing something for yourself. Depending on your age and shape, you will need to begin with something very light. I would encourage you to even seek the advice of your doctor before starting an exercise program. A personal trainer can also be extremely helpful in guiding you.

Another important part of your physical regiment is, of course, your diet. Just like with your car, if bad information is put into the memory chip, the car will not function at full capacity. Or consider how with computers, garbage going in will ensure garbage coming out. Your diet will change over the years, and the needs of your body will change with your age. This is important to accept. The nutrients that you place in your body today may result in a bad outcome tomorrow. Keep in mind that just like with mental and spiritual health, physical health is different for everyone. You have to identify what works for you and not get caught up in trying to look like a bodybuilder to be in recognizably good shape. You do not need to be able to run a marathon or lift a couple hundred pounds to be in good physical condition. If you start yourself on a nutritious diet and exercise to enable greater use of your body, your mind will be energized.

The last part of the triad is your spiritual health. I am sure you have heard that "it is better to give than it is to receive." This is true, and you can feel incredible personal pride by finding ways to give to others. There is always someone in need of assistance in our society, and you can show that you volunteer your time to set a good example. When others see that you are a caring individual, you will earn their respect. Take a look around you. How many spirits are being uplifted from people going to work and making money? For most, this is necessary to have the things you need and want in life. Nonetheless, a simple act of kindness will replicate in those who see you do it.

A Visual Example of Faith Leadership

As I write this, my family is celebrating the life of a special person, Pansy Samuels Taylor McDaniel. At ninety-three years old, she was still strong in her spiritual faith. She knew she was moving on to a better place after suffering through a stroke and many years of dealing with dementia. She was, and is, a shining example of spiritual health to everyone who involved her in their lives. She had a positive impact on my life, and I will always carry her with me. Pansy was Cheryl's grandmother.

I have known my wife since the eighth grade. We did not start dating until our senior year of high school, and when we did, life moved quickly from prom, to graduation, to boot camp, and finally to marriage. Thirty-two years later, we continue to grow strong together due to the amazing foundations we have both been given at home in our faith and love for God and family. I will never forget the day I took Pansy's oldest grandchild, and only granddaughter, away from Greene County, Virginia, to Mississippi. She was standing on her country house's porch, and she looked at Cheryl, aware that I was standing right next to her granddaughter. She told Cheryl, "If he ever hurts you, you better let me know so that I can take care of it." It was like she was telling me that she had a posse on standby to go get the man who could hurt her only granddaughter. I heard her loud and clear, and her words kept me focused.

I can never remember a time in her life when she talked negatively about anyone. If she disagreed with someone, she just smiled, as if to say, "We are not going to have an argument." She did not judge; she only served others and in turn showed them how they could live a happy and fulfilled life of serving others. Deeply rooted in her faith, she attended church whenever services were provided. When her church family needed her, she offered them her support. She knew that they too were her family. She also knew that this was how God wanted her to live her life.

At the memorial services celebrating Pansy's life, the pastor mentioned that no one could ever question Pansy's faith or commitment. She had lived by example, and she had touched many people during her lifetime. This was obvious by the size of the crowd that day. She had also therefore been a leader to the many who surrounded her. She had exemplified spiritual health. Spiritual health had given her, and others, the resolve and mission to serve in life. It had allowed her to not focus on or worry about the negative things that often-burdened others in life. She had had inner happiness, a special smile, and an incredible faith. She had been on a path set by God, and she had done only her very best to serve others.

Cheryl often jokes about how I won over Pansy—or Granny, as we all called her. We were playing around at a family gathering when I nudged Cheryl, and she said, "Granny, did you see what he did to me?"

"What?" her grandmother asked.

Cheryl said, "He pushed me."

Granny's reply was, "Well, maybe you deserved it."

At that point, I knew I was safe from the posse and that Granny was confident that I had taken care of, and would continue to take care of, her granddaughter. I cannot tell you the joy that knowledge brought to my heart. You never fully understand to what degree people have shaped your life until they are no longer with you. With Granny, however, we always knew her love and kindness were making us all stronger. Thank you, Granny. You are missed but never forgotten.

Remain Positive, Even During a Negative Experience

As a leader of a team, it is important for you to be supportive and encourage your team through active communication. There is, of course, the need to communicate expectations and update your team with new information. However, you must also ensure you spend time publicly praising the efforts of your team, and you must always counsel them in private. As you respect those you lead, they will develop respect for you. I learned this lesson early in my navy career.

I was a very junior second class petty officer on board USS *Comte de Grasse* (DD 974), and we were returning to port. I was placed in a leadership position over an entire division. Part of our division's responsibility while returning the ship to home port was to set up the quarterdeck, which is the ship's primary entrance in port. Our team also placed large rubber fenders over the side of the ship when we pulled in to protect it from being damaged against the pier. I was in charge of this function, and one of my junior sailors decided to leave his station as we were delayed in returning. He failed to return in time for our final entry pier side, and so his fender did not make it over the side of the ship in time. Thankfully, we did not suffer any damage, but I was furious with the sailor for what could have occurred. When he did return, my anger got the best of me; I confronted him in a very angry manner in front of a group of other people. In my young leader's mind, I thought I was setting a standard in dealing with him in front of the others. However, what really occurred was that I lost all the respect of that individual, and it was very difficult for me to motivate him into any action afterward. Everyone knew he was wrong—even he knew he was wrong—but what I did not see was that I was wrong in the way I handled it.

Learning such a significant lesson has guided me throughout my career. That sailor taught me a very valuable lesson, and it stuck. People make mistakes—this is a fact of life. How you, as a leader, handle a negative experience and whether you can turn it into a positive experience may just determine the level of respect you receive from everyone. I did later apologize to the sailor when giving him written counseling, but the damage had been done, and those around us may have lost a little respect for me as well.

Always Take the Opportunity to Recognize Good

If you are willing to counsel someone to resolve negativity, be willing to also counsel that person on the positive aspects of his or her performance. What I always felt was underutilized in the navy is meritorious captain's mast. Captain's mast on a ship is a procedure in which the commanding officer holds crew members accountable for their mistakes. However, every commanding officer also has the option to have a meritorious captain's mast to recognize outstanding performance. This is done in front of the sailor's peers, similar to an award ceremony. It is an alternative way for the commanding officer to express appreciation for a job well done.

Think about the opportunities you have to recognize outstanding performance where you work and seek to do so in front of others. And think about how you handle negative situations in general. It is often the ways in which you handle the negative situations that will define you as a leader, as they are the ones everyone is watching. Will they still respect you after you manage a negative situation with them? Never forget that a team is always watching their leaders. Do your team members still want to be like you, or did they just learn how *not* to handle a similar situation? You have a choice, and you should often think about how you will choose to handle these situations. You are only their leader if they view you as their leader—and not because you have the title.

Seek Feedback to Improve as a Positive Leader

Make sure that you are the type of leader our future demands. Accomplish this through self-evaluation and by considering the feedback of your own leaders and mentors. Leaders at all levels must learn to value self-evaluation and mentorship. If you asked any successful leader, I would be willing to bet you that this person admired and sought advice from someone while he or she was developing. It is important for your team to see this in your actions and hear it from you often. A huge part of your character originates from how you were developed and how you achieved your level of knowledge and overall success. Letting your team see that you consistently seek their guidance, and that you often reach out to your mentors for their advice on how to deal with new situations and evolve as a leader, will enable them to see that they need to value these practices themselves.

Take a few minutes to stop and think about those who have contributed to your development and who you continue to lean on for support. Write a paragraph about each one of these important people and then use them as examples when you want to teach those you lead. If you are sharing your important life lessons with your team, they will feel that you are making a positive investment in them, and you will therefore show them that you must continue to use your resources to learn and develop. Leadership is a learning journey that does not end. Every day offers a new situation with a new opportunity to improve.

Every Team Member Is a Leader

We started this chapter with the concept of projecting a positive attitude, and it is important to finish on the same point. In life, your attitude affects your environment as well as everyone around you. Whether you are at home, at work, or simply walking down the street, you can change lives just with the way you project yourself. Here is another opportunity to reflect and assess. Positivity is infectious, and so is negativity. Which one will you project, and which one will your organization's environment reflect?

In the navy, we expect the commanding officer to be responsible for the command climate. While I do agree with this practice, I also believe that everyone on the team has a responsibility to improve and promote a positive organization. I always considered every sailor on the team, from the most junior to the most senior, a leader. As leaders, we all have to contribute by working to ensure that our organization is on the right path. If you do not understand this, it is time to do a self-evaluation and decide what you can do to make a difference. Maybe the problem is not with the organization but with how you perceive it. There is only one person who can shape your perception and that is you. Work to develop your team and improve the overall climate through your leadership at your level. You have the opportunity, and only you can make the decision to make a difference.

POP Points

- You always have the opportunity to influence others.
- You control your internal pride meter.
- Maintaining a healthy lifestyle includes maintaining your mind, body, and spirit.
- It is better to give than to receive.
- A simple act of kindness that you display will be replicated by others.
- How you handle a negative situation can also impact how others view you as a leader.
- Get feedback from other leaders and mentors to assist you in your self-evaluation.

CHAPTER 7

Success Education

HAVE YOU EVER noticed that when your organization wants to train you to perform a specific task at work, the training is a process or regulation to help you? However, when it comes to a social behavioral issue, people tend to show you the negative outcome of that behavior to keep you from replicating it. A good example of this is how society, and even the navy, expends a great amount of resources to show everyone what may occur if they drink and drive. Possible outcomes include causing an accident, being arrested, securing an under-the-influence conviction, and earning insurance increases. All these things happen, and they are all deterrents to keep you from making this poor decision. However, how many commercials have you seen showing you how not to put yourself in that situation?

Educating by Leading Success

There have been some changes over time to how this is approached, but there always seems to be this parental lecture telling you how bad the outcome will be versus showing you how to not get into the situation in the first place. Reflect on this yourself: When you were a young person, how often did you actually listen to the parental lectures? I recall a presentation from my time on active duty in which paramedics got up on a stage and used an egg to demonstrate what would happen to the body in an accident. They proceeded to show what it would be like when medical professionals had to stick all kinds of instruments into the body to repair it, causing extreme pain.

It is not always necessary for you to focus on negative aspects when educating your team members on areas of concern. In fact, I started to emphasize educating on the positive factors to avoid these areas. Few people desire to address that alcohol is a problem in our society. For over thirty years, I have seen how it can play a major role in ending many careers and lives. Societal drinking is a reality, but how do we show that it can be done responsibly so that everyone can remain a productive and successful member of our teams? I believe the way to do this is to have others model the proper behavior of responsible drinking. It is key to show how the alcohol may act on someone's body and the impairment that may follow. We can teach people that they must always have transportation plans or a designated driver. Using a performance counseling session model, we can start by pointing out the positive aspects of the person's performance. We can then point out any weaknesses and end with making a plan for improvement.

I have always been extremely proud of my former chief petty officer's mess on USS *George Washington*. They engaged with and worked to support our sailors. As we conducted port visits overseas, we wanted to ensure a successful deployment in all areas to include our Sailors going on liberty and addressing this as a mission. Being successful on liberty was just as important as being successful in our combat missions. Alcohol was always a concern overseas as the drinking age was generally eighteen versus twenty-one at home. There were many new experiences with alcohol overseas for Sailors who had never consumed alcohol before. During port visits, events were held on the pier. This gave the sailors the option to stay close to the ship. In some places, such as Jebel Ali, we used the term *beer on the pier.* These events were often run with little control, and the focus was on making money for the morale fund for future events. I approached our chiefs with my thoughts on the practice, and they bought into a different tactic. Carrier Air Wing Seven was aboard, and they joined the effort as one unified group of chiefs. I was proud of what Command Master Chief Eric Williamson and I were able to achieve in bringing the team together, across command lines. The unity that he and I displayed promoted the expectation that we would all work as one.

The chiefs (senior enlisted) aboard the ship took charge of the Beer on the Pier program. We established a process whereby a sailor could purchase two beers at a time and educated the crew on how they could do so. We wanted a chief to look each sailor in the eye when they all bought beer to ensure that they were OK, so the chiefs controlled the sales. We even had twenty-five chiefs walking the area that had been set up with tables and chairs, and we provided live music for a more relaxing atmosphere. The chiefs controlled security in the area and ensured that everyone behaved. This program was so successful that various other groups of officers wanted to join in and support the events with the chiefs. People typically want to be a part of a good thing.

What did we learn from this evolution? Sailors loved these events, and instead of going out into town to drink, they stayed close to the ship, as they felt that they were being taken care of. If a sailor showed signs of having had too much to drink, he or she was escorted back to the ship by a chief and not allowed to depart again that evening. We also learned that our efforts were showing our sailors how to take care of each other when they were drinking away from the ship. They knew to bring someone back or call for help from shore patrol—the onboard personnel serving as safety—or security patrols on liberty if they needed assistance. The chiefs learned that we could better account for the alcohol and the funds, as we made a much larger profit with this process in place. It was a very proud moment for our entire crew—including the air wing and battle group staff—when we were about to end our deployment and realized that we had encountered zero liberty incidents while overseas. Thus, and most importantly, we learned that success can depend on whether leaders are engaged and working to be a part of the solution instead of ignoring the issue. It's all about showing your people that you truly care for them by sacrificing your personal time to ensure their success, as all our chiefs did on our ship.

Another important concept is that success may be replicated when the people you are leading see you as an engaged leader and therefore learn from your positive leadership. They will also ultimately replicate your success at various leadership levels throughout the organization. If you discuss only the negative aspects of their work, you are projecting negativity, and that may be all they understand. If you want them to follow your positive behavior, you must first show them success. In all situations, they need to see the good and not the bad. Once you show them how to lead, you must provide them the opportunity to do so. The chiefs on USS *George Washington* were outstanding, and they taught me a great deal about leadership. I would later translate these lessons into the development of a program used to engage young sailors, while I served as the Navy Region Mid-Atlantic command master chief.

Educating Leadership to Inspire Success

Rear Admiral Mark Boensel was my region commander while assigned as the region command master chief. He was a very engaged leader, and I learned valuable lessons from him that enabled me to grow. Later, in chapter 12, I will discuss how our interaction led to the creation of a peer-to-peer mentoring group in which I was able to apply much of what I had learned on USS *George Washington*. I would now like to share with you how he worked to improve the effectiveness of leadership on his team through reading and open discussion.

On active duty, you develop in a culture in which leadership training is required as you progress through the ranks. In the civilian ranks, however, that opportunity is very limited. Our civilian workforce at Navy Region Mid-Atlantic was outstanding. As we conducted our mandatory command climate surveys with the workforce, it was easy to identify from comments the civilian workforce had provided that they felt they were not getting much needed leadership training at all levels. Of course, we had financial constraints, which kept us from being able to provide outside training sources. But Rear Admiral Boensel knew we could overcome this obstacle and achieve both growth and unity through an in-house process. He shared one of his previous experiences of teaching leadership from within the organization with Executive Director Fred Crecelious, Chief of Staff Captain Pearson, and I.

His direction was to separate all enlisted, officer, and civilian leaders into three groups titled Red, White, and Blue. These groups would include each type of leader so that we could enable growth and understanding across all levels of leadership. Once that had been done, he bought every leader *The 21 Irrefutable Laws of Leadership,* by John Maxwell, and gave them the next month to read the book. We then started to schedule days of the week for each group, during which we would bring them into the conference room for popcorn, soda, and a movie. Our goal in these sessions was to show them an episode of the *Band of Brothers* miniseries, which took about fifty minutes. They were given sheets of paper that listed the various laws from the book, and as they watched, they took notes to identify which of those laws were utilized in the series. Upon completion of the episode, Real Admiral Boensel personally led a discussion on how the laws were exercised. The interaction and the various perspectives were incredible, and they enabled everyone to learn about leadership while also removing barriers across the various leadership teams.

Rear Admiral Boensel shared with us all a story of success about learning leadership without a significant financial investment. While we may have been resource constrained and thus unable to provide any official funded leadership training, we were still able to learn great lessons of leadership just by talking to one another. As you can imagine, as our leader led the team through this process, everyone developed not only trust but also a better understanding of leadership expectations. We were still not perfect, but we were stronger together.

Inspiration for Success Comes from Many Unexpected Places

I would like to share another very personal story with you that I call "The Cody Story." As I write this, I am sitting on an airplane departing Orlando, Florida, to return to my home in Stafford, Virginia. I always look forward to going home and spending time with Cheryl and our two dogs, Cody and Molly. However, this trip will be different, and the anxiety I am feeling is terrible. This time, when I return home, we will be taking Cody to our veterinarian office, and he will not be coming back with us.

Just as I reflect on my dad every day, and on the many gifts he gave me in life, I know I will also recall the many gifts that Cody has given me. Our pets become part of our families. For many people, pets are the only children they will ever have. Cheryl and I are fortunate to have two amazing sons, but our puppies filled a gap in our lives when our boys moved on to their own lives. In fact, I would often tell people that Cody and Molly were our so-called kid replacement program. Anthony and Jason always appreciated that statement. Cody was our family's first dog, and he is—and will always be—very special.

As previously stated, I have used the story of the importance of positive reinforcement to training our two dogs in many leadership discussions. If you want your dog to do a trick, give them a treat when they do it, and they will forever respond to your command in pursuit of that treat. On the other hand, if you get upset and kick the dog for not performing the trick, the dog is likely to bite you in response. This just goes to show you once again that you will get the behavior that you give. Training a dog is all about executing leadership, the art of influence. In the same respect, if you expect a positive response from those around you, then you should project a positive presentation of yourself. I have learned many other lessons from Cody. We often take this for granted when it happens, but I know that God sent Cody to me to teach me some very important life lessons. The two most important came through the unconditional love and loyalty that he gave to me. If you are a dog owner, you know exactly what I am talking about. There is no other species on Earth willing to forgive you when you have done something wrong to them like your dog always does. They work so hard to obtain your love and affection that they truly, and very quickly, forget the past— especially if you are willing to show them that affection.

Their loyalty is incredible. As I would get ready to walk out the door for work every day, Cody would come to the door and see me off. Many times, he would even whine because he did not want me to go. He would also lay at the same door every night to protect us. Cody is a chow chow-golden retriever mix. He was always in protection mode; whether in the house or in the yard, he was protecting all of us. When Molly wanted to play with him, he would often fuss at her as if to tell her she was preventing him from carrying out his role and responsibilities as the protector. As a sailor, I can understand his concern. He was a great watch stander, and I am grateful to know that he will now be watching from above. When I would come home from work, he would hear the loud exhaust of my Mustang and be watching out the window to see me pull into the driveway. He would then excitedly meet me at the garage door, his tail wagging. I was always excited to see him as well.

Cheryl once asked me, "Why are you not that excited to see me when you get home?"

My response was, "Well, if you met me at the door with your tail wagging, maybe I would be." You can imagine how that went over.

Cody has brought tremendous joy to our lives. The fact that we have to make the decision to end his life is very painful but also necessary to end his suffering. Yes, the tears are flowing, and there is an ache in my heart that will not go away. Somehow, I know that the pressure will cease once the procedure has been completed. Just as it was a relief to know that my dad was not suffering with his pancreatic cancer anymore, I know there will be relief in knowing that my Cody Bear is no longer suffering. I love you, Bear. Rest easy, and always know that I am grateful to have shared my life with you, and that you now join my dad to watch over us. You have made me a better person. You were eternally proud to protect and happy to be with us. Your outlook on life and your desire to serve our family has had a tremendously positive impact on me. You led me more than you will ever know. Rest in peace, shipmate. I have the watch and will execute it well due to the lessons that only you could teach me.

Just as my dad inspired me to continue to pursue the development of **POP** Leadership in his last year with us, Cody will now become the inspiration that has me working to complete this book. We all need something to keep us motivated and focused on the positives in life, especially during our toughest times. Cody's loss has hit me very hard. His memory will now drive me to recall the good times he shared with me and my family and the positive impact he had on all our lives. You can learn leadership from many in life, and I hope this story shows how important our pets are to us. If you have never had a dog, I encourage you to go to a local shelter and adopt one. We rescued Cody from the SPCA in Norfolk, Virginia, and our life lessons began immediately. Love a dog, and learn and grow together.

As you look at this special picture of Cody on the day before his departure, ask yourself this question: Which do you want your team members to emulate, success or failure? Which are you projecting through your actions? Which are you presenting as you prepare them for their future actions?

Success or Failure?

When you sought out other leaders for their mentorship, did you ask them how they failed or how they succeeded? Of course, I know the response. When you are pursuing success, why would you ever want to spend any amount of time discussing failure? Yes, it is necessary to talk about past mistakes, but only insofar as you understand how you overcame them, learned from them, and applied that knowledge to a successful process. Teach your team success and watch them lead success. Failing to teach them properly, or spending too much time focused on the negative aspects, may just get you what you are giving them.

POP Points

- Showing your team that you are willing to sacrifice your personal time for their success ensures their trust in you.
- If you want others to follow your positive behavior, you must first show them success.
- You will get the behavior you give.
- Having something positive to focus on in a negative situation can enable us to develop and improve our understanding.
- Teach them success and watch them lead success. Show them how to fail, even if only to deter them, and failure may be their response.

Recommended reading: *The 21 Irrefutable Laws of Leadership*, by John C. Maxwell.

USS *George Washington* (CVN 73)

Commanding Officer Captain Martin Erdossy III, Executive Officer Captain Dee Mewbourne, and Command Master Chief Scott Benning on the USS *George Washington* flight deck during the 2004 deployment to the Middle East

Fleet Master Chief Scott Benning with his sons Scott "Anthony" Benning Jr. and Jason Benning at the Naval Station Norfolk 2012 Coalition of Sailors Against Destructive Decision (CSADD) rally

USS *George Washington* Command Master Chief Scott Benning

USS *George Washington* Command Master Chief Scott Benning making
Commanding Officer Marty Erdossy an honorary chief petty officer

USS *George Washington* Command Master Chief Scott
Benning with Newport News Mayor Joe S. Frank

Retired Master Chief Petty Officer of the Navy Rick West
with Retired Fleet Master Chief Scott Benning, visiting the
office of the master chief petty officer of the navy.

POP Leadership Artwork by Robert Passley

CHAPTER 8

————— ⟨⟨⟨⟩⟩⟩ —————

Understanding Influence

Leaders Are Developed, Not Born

HAVE YOU EVER thought about how and when we, as individuals, start to develop influencing behaviors? If you have children, I'm sure you give this a great deal of thought every day. Think about it: when you have a newborn child who is hungry, he or she will cry. Why do babies do this? He or she demands your attention. You absolutely hate to see your child cry, so what do you do? You investigate the situation. When did he or she last eat? The baby should not be hungry yet, so maybe he or she has a wet diaper. You do all you can to make sure you are meeting the needs of your newborn child. So, if he or she cries when they are hungry and you feed them, the baby will know exactly how to get the necessary response the next time they are hungry or need a new diaper. Yes, the baby is leading you to change your behavior to meet his or her needs. Leadership is all about having influence, so even as a baby, your child is developing influence.

This may not be the way you want to view changing behavior as your child gets older. Naturally, you will start to recognize that the child is capable of doing things on his or her own, and you will be relieved of many tasks. Who wants to change the diapers of a ten-year-old unless the child has a disability of some sort? So, when your child can perform a task for him- or herself, you will start to influence his or her behavior.

Mentoring and Influencing Success

My grandson is in the midst of potty training, and my wife has helped mentor our son and daughter-in-law with the lessons she learned while teaching our kids. Yes, she is mentoring the new parents by helping them to learn what she already knows. If you want the kid to perform a trick, you must reward him for doing so. Punishing or yelling at your child for not doing what you want them to do is going to take a lot more time and negative energy than it would to reward them for a job well done. When our son and daughter-in-law first struggled with this process, Cole would cry in disappointment, sensing that his mom and dad were unhappy with him. It was stressful for all of them.

Cheryl shared an idea with them. She suggested that they buy a calendar and some stickers. She told them that every time her boys had used the potty, she had given them a sticker to put on the calendar the day of the event to see how many they could get. The positive reinforcement made it less about going to the potty and more about getting a sticker to put on the calendar. Anthony and Darcie followed her suggestion, and they soon realized that their little Cole man loves his stickers, and he looked for one each time he went to the bathroom. It all sounds crazy, does it not?

We can track our behaviors all the way back to our earliest days in life. Leaders are not born; they are taught to be positive or negative leaders. Of course, they can change when they are capable of seeing the advantages and disadvantages of the two perspectives. Which type of leader are you, and what do you find most effective?

Leading Your Leaders

Think about how your child influenced your behavior first. Some would say that the child understood early on in life that he or she could influence someone else. This is a point we sometimes forget as we progress through life and join various teams. Do you lead those you work for? I personally believe that not only do we perform this task but we have the responsibility to lead our leaders to ensure that our teams are as effective as they can be. Yes, you learn from your leaders. But the greatest leaders will also learn from those they lead. As you develop future leaders, ensure that you are also supporting those you work for so that they too will develop. You may have knowledge that they do not, and that knowledge can enable them to grow.

Negativity or Positivity: Which Influences Your Actions?

As you were growing up, you were likely, at one time or another, a member of some type of team—a sports team or academic team, for example. Did you just sit back and let everyone else tell you what to do? Or did you adapt to make the team stronger and ensure that they understood your point of view? If you were successful, I am sure the latter applies. If you had a negative leader who did not want to listen to you, did you want to stay on that team or move on to another team? If the coach yelled at you all the time for doing something wrong and never invested in you by teaching you how to improve, did you enjoy the experience? I am pretty confident you did not like that team and probably looked for a way to get off it. However, if you were struggling with something and the coach or teacher invested the time in you to make you stronger, you probably viewed that coach or teacher as the best one you had ever had. They saw your capability, and they invested in you so that you could develop. Who would not want to be around a person like that? Often, we think someone is chasing us away because of his or her style. It is important to realize that, just like the newborn baby, we have the opportunity to change the leader's behavior through our influence.

Whether you have a positive or a negative leader, you have the opportunity to decide how you will react to and influence their conduct. Take the time to learn about the leader and then initiate discussions about leadership development that can help you both to become stronger for the benefit of your team. Seek opportunities to discuss POP Leadership with leaders at all levels to ensure that your positive energy can be felt by all. You will feel better about yourself, and others will start to lean on you. You will be promoting an environment that others will want to be a part of. You will become a leader to many more on your team because of your infectious positive energy. As you invest in others and provide a positive influence, you are showing all leaders how their actions and overall leadership can have a positive impact on others.

Leading Through Followership

Another very important aspect of being a leader is followership. You must first understand the importance of following if you expect to lead and influence others. There are very few in life, if any, who do not work for someone else or a body of people in the execution of their responsibilities. In a larger sense, leaders must realize that they work for those they lead. However, if you want your team members to trust and follow you, you must be willing to show them that you can follow as well.

Imagine this scenario: a team leader is given a problem for his leaders to solve, but the leader has routinely presented this problem to the team as a senseless issue. The behavior that you model for your team members will most likely lead to the same behavior in them. As a leader, you do not have the luxury of picking and choosing when you want to lead. You do not have the luxury of venting to another team member. And if your leader presents you with a problem that you do not believe in, you have the opportunity to influence your leader. If you are unable to do this and your leader still demands that the issue be addressed, you must own this and take the issue to your team as if it were your own idea to do so. Do not present the issue to your team in a manner that degrades its importance, but rather present the importance of working through the issue together. You do not need to share with your team that you do not believe your boss gave you a valuable task. You had your chance to change the boss's decision. And now you may need to evaluate how you can present your case differently to those you lead.

Supporting Your Leadership When They Need You Most

As a fleet master chief, I had the opportunity to work for a great leader. At the time, he was Vice Admiral (three-star admiral) Mark Ferguson, but he eventually became Admiral (four-star admiral) Ferguson. As the chief of naval personnel, he was presented with a significant task: he had to reduce the workforce to reflect our level of funding after Congress had made various cuts. The chief of naval operations, his boss, had communicated that there was no available funding to help retain the current level of manning across the navy. Neither leader wanted to execute this task, but it was necessary both to stay within authorized funding levels and to not impact the readiness—or future readiness—of our navy.

Vice Admiral Ferguson worked hard with our team, for an extended period of time, to find ways of identifying funding. In fact, in previous years, he had led efforts to avoid doing what he now had to. When he understood that we could not change our course, he took ownership of the actions necessary to complete the task. He did not blame his leader for not finding resources. He led the efforts of our team, and the Enlisted Continuation Board was assembled for the first time since the end of the Korean War. In the early seventies, over thirty thousand sailors had been directed to depart the navy as it had been necessary to downsize after the conflict. In 2008, it became necessary to do the same though on a much smaller scale; three thousand sailors were let go.

This was a painstaking effort that no one wanted to take on. We all understood the impact that this action would have on sailors and their families. Due to these impacts, special authorities are required and were authorized by congress to enable this to occur. The team worked diligently, over a very long period of time and with the input of many, to ensure that this task was executed as fairly as possible. I can recall few times when Vice Admiral Ferguson would visit my office versus those when I was asked to visit his. It was during this time that I could see his anxiety. He needed to be able to talk about this while also maintaining a level of integrity and respect for how we executed the necessary actions. As a leader, you are not presented with easy issues. If the issues were easy, would they really need you as the leader? Leaders must make the tough decisions, and they must consider the potential outcomes of their actions.

This period was, without a doubt, one of the most difficult times of my tour. However, I was grateful to have a great leader in Admiral Ferguson, who was successfully leading our team and asking all the necessary questions. He provided a terrific example of listening, learning, and leading for us all. He listened to the concerns and recommendations of leaders at all levels in the navy, from the most junior to the most senior of sailors. From their input, he learned how to better execute the process. He then led our team in developing and implementing the policy from beginning to end. At the same time, he was also making sure that communications were maximized across the navy to keep all informed. This enabled those who would be asked to leave to prepare as soon as possible. Many today see Admiral Ferguson as a quiet leader. I considered him a heavy thinker and compassionate leader who understood leadership better than most. After all, it is during the most difficult times that you learn the most about leadership, and he was undoubtedly—and continues to be—a great leader to emulate.

Learning and Developing

Your actions today can have a huge influence on the future when you understand that people respond to positivity. Life has a way of teaching lessons that shape you as a person. These are the lessons that influence your behavior and attitude and therefore help you to understand influence in many shapes and forms. In life, you tend to base your direction and how you will approach new situations on what you have learned in the past. Yes, your past shapes you so that you can progress, and when you learn life lessons, gaining insight and guidance from those you trust, you reach new levels of success. I have used many such lessons to evaluate myself and adjust my priorities, both personal and professional. You can often get overwhelmed and lose focus on the things that are most important to you. This past year has given me new opportunities to review my life and reshape my priorities.

Knowing Your Priorities to Influence Your Decisions

Cheryl is the largest influence in my life as she truly guides me. This has helped me to realize why our nation places so much emphasis on not just the presidential candidate but also the candidate's spouse. Those who have strong marriages know that the spouse often has an impact on how the couple are shaped and how the decisions are made. Our families help shape us and influence our actions. You can see this in recent presidential spouses. Nancy Reagan was known to have a huge influence in many areas of Ronald Reagan's presidency. And think about the impact that Barbara Bush has had on our nation, with her husband as president and the son she raised. When you look at the Bush family, you see a family of service—one who have great respect for all.

As a veteran, I cannot think of any other presidents who have shown more love and support for their service members than these two. Do you think Nancy and Barbara had something to do with this? Absolutely they did. They led their families to understand the importance of serving others and thus their ability to influence others and even change the course of our nation. Of course, many other presidential spouses have followed suit. Most recently, Michelle Obama has implemented efforts to support military service members and families. All these spouses have earned trust and developed influence as they have focused on serving others. They made the concept of serving others a priority within their families to inspire success.

Today, as I write this, I am sitting in the waiting room while Cheryl is in surgery to have a kidney stone removed. I have never experienced a kidney stone, and after watching her go through this and hearing her say that the pain is worse than childbirth, I hope I never have to. It is tough to watch a loved one in so much pain. Deciding whether I should go to work or stay by her side while she is ill may seem difficult. She is the example I have worked to emulate. She has been amazing for her family this past year. Her mom has been dealing with cancer, and as I conveyed earlier, her grandmother's passing has been trying. You never know someone's true strength until they are challenged with the most difficult life situations, and Cheryl has been a true champion in every sense. I have learned a great deal from her example and making sure that I am here to take care of her is the only decision for me as I have watched her do the same for many other family members. Many times, we get caught up in whether we have enough leave or the option to take time off. I have come to realize that there is nothing more important in life than my wife. The rest will take care of itself. I need to take care of her in the manner that she has always taken care of me and everyone else. You get what you give in life, and right now, she needs me to be my best self so that I can take care of her.

Over the past year, I have also evaluated my personal interests and works. Anthony and Darcie have blessed us with our second grandson. We now have two amazing grandsons, Cole and Hunter. Brianna introduced us to our first beautiful granddaughter, Evelyn, and she and Jason also expanded their family with the wonderful addition of Gracelyn. As our families grow, the need to be there for our family also grows. I have had to take a look at the many extra things I am doing in life to shift my priorities to reflect what I have always preached: family first. I recently resigned as a vice president of a nonprofit company and will later end my fourth term on its board of directors. Being a leader in various organizations and giving back to so many is very rewarding, but I understand that my priorities must shift. I also know that I must give others the opportunity to lead while I work to focus more on my family.

I have done a lot of talking about my personal decisions, but what I hope I have shown you is that you should take an annual look at your priorities and goals. Ask yourself if you are focusing the necessary energy on the things you most desire. Think about those who influenced you and how they have shaped you. Are you applying what you have learned to increase the satisfaction in your life while you meet your objectives?

What brings the most joy to your life? For me, it is the love of my family. When I place that priority first, I am living a happy life. I have my wife to thank for keeping me focused, and as the medical staff work to relieve her pain from the kidney stones today, I am exactly where I need to be—with her and caring for her. Ask yourself: Are you where you need to be?

Building Trust and Influence

Understand that trust is not given to you along with a title; it is developed and earned through the professional relationships you have with those around you.

I have a suspicion that writing a book was easier years ago, with a typewriter and correction tape. Today, the use of technology would make you believe that word processing programs make this easier and quicker. Although this may be true in some sense, a great deal of learning must take place in order to utilize technology. This too displays the simple fact that life is a learning journey and that, to be relevant in any given task, you must be willing to learn new ways to influence and communicate with others.

So here I sit on the train, writing about utilizing a new technology called the iPad. It is already becoming old technology as people seek ways to regenerate the hardware with new software. This can be compared to what is happening in your workforce. Humans are living longer than ever; the average age of the workforce continues to increase, and many are working longer in life before deciding to retire. In many ways, the aging hardware that we utilize to complete necessary work will require new software. This is accomplished by preparing the aging workforce through the learning process to improve their production and thus continue to be an asset to your team. The hardware's passion and desire to contribute have not changed. However, the leader needs to understand the challenges that the hardware may have when using the new software and how the two must work together to make the team stronger.

Your team members do not care what your title is; they only want their leader to give them the tools and knowledge they need to succeed. Just as you cannot write software that requires advanced technology and then utilize it on aging hardware, you cannot expect your aging workforce to easily adapt to new technology. How you influence your team's proficiency with the new technology will be a major factor in your success.

Retention is something we do as adult learners through repetition of a task or by conducting open communications to learn. Expecting the old hardware to read a book and thereby learn to adapt to new software is not often going to get you good results. How many times have you seen someone depart a job because they were deemed unable to adapt to change? Perhaps we leaders need to look at what we are doing to support and influence their adaptation to new technology. In some cases, the problem may not be with the hardware but rather the technician, pushing the software. It is important for you, as the technician (leader), to understand how you can support and influence the hardware, or the new user of the software (technology). The leader must educate the new user as to how their efforts can impact the system you expect them to adapt to.

Technology is important, but in the end, it is the people who are getting the work done. When you lose your focus on the people, you are treading dangerous ground. Yes, people can be replaced; however, creating a culture in which the technology is more important than the people will cause you to lose the respect of your workforce. This may lead you down a negative path and result in your having degraded relationships with everyone around you. Managing the transition from something old to something new will require a great deal of care and communication. Ensure that your leadership team are making the necessary plans to implement prior to this transition. You will have greater acceptance and success with the proper preparation. If you are poor in your planning and communications, you will ultimately fail.

As you think about the word *influence*, it seems pretty simple in definition. However, when you turn it into an action in your life, you will start to realize that it takes a tremendous amount of work and know-how to be able to develop both your leadership abilities and your influence. Leaders are not born; they are made as they learn from life lessons. Some may even be made into leaders due to some financial or other social status. But they do not truly become leaders unless they learn the many lessons of leadership along the journey we call life. Life is a learning journey, and each day, you are working to develop yourself into a stronger person and therefore a stronger leader.

POP Points

- Great leaders learn from those they lead.
- As you invest in others and provide them positive influence, you also show all leaders that their actions can have a positive impact on others.
- Followership is an important leadership trait to pass on to those you lead.
- Put family first!
- Our families help shape us and influence our actions.
- You get what you give in life.
- Trust and the ability to influence others are not given to you along with a title; both are developed through the professional relationships that you have with those around you.
- Leaders are not born; they learn to lead through life lessons.

Recommended reading: *The 360 Degree Leader*, by John C. Maxwell.

CHAPTER 9

—— ⬥ ——

Creating an Environment of Giving and Caring

THERE ARE MANY aspects to promoting a positive climate within your organization. Leaders often look at others when a problem arises, but in reality, they need only to look within themselves.

Rebuilding Success When Failure Occurs

During my time as the command master chief aboard USS *George Washington*, our command triad worked very hard to promote a positive climate for our crew. We focused on leadership to ensure that we were doing all that we could to enable the success of all our sailors. Of course, there were times when mistakes were made. How you handle such situations as a leader can have a huge impact on how the others perceive the environment. We all make mistakes in life, and I am confident that most understand that some mistakes require more accountability than others. However, when one is held accountable, he or she should be given the same level of respect as any other individual to enable them to overcome the mistake and have an opportunity for future success. The manner in which a leader handles this can have a huge impact on how well the individual is able to overcome the shortfalls and create future success for the team.

When you have a large population of young people on your team, you are faced with many challenges, as many mistakes are made. One issue that we faced in the navy was our sailors getting tickets for driving under the influence of alcohol. We had worked hard to increase awareness on the impacts of this mistake, but of course, on occasion, it would still occur. The sailors faced accountability in the courts, but we wanted them to know that we still cared for them. We wanted to make them understand that we did not want them to repeat the same mistakes.

When sailors returned to duty, they would come to my office with their department leaders. We would have the sailor walk us through the day of the incident and the decisions they had made leading up to it. We also discussed what it was like to be arrested and the many ways that this would impact them, personally and financially. Hopefully their bad decision had not impacted anyone else. Again, I wanted all sailors to know that we cared about them and wanted them to learn from and overcome their mistake. In an effort to ensure that they did not repeat the mistake, they were given a homework assignment that was due in my office the following morning. They were all required to write a letter to their next of kin. That may have been their spouses, their parents or guardians, or even their kids. They were to write the letter as though they had just been killed in an accident as the result of drinking and driving. They were to express their regret for their actions and for ignoring all that our command had done to prevent them from making this terrible decision.

The sailors were also required to provide any suggestions on how we could improve our efforts to discourage others from making the same mistake. I shared with them that I would be keeping their letters in my desk just in case they had not learned from their mistake and continued with their bad behavior. I told them that if this did occur, I would send their letters to their next of kin to show their families that we cared about our sailors, that we were doing all we could to communicate to them how important it is to make good decisions, and that they still made bad decisions. I wanted those sailors to realize the impact that their actions had on their families. I wanted to learn from them what we could have done differently to make them understand that they needed to have a plan in place to avoid driving under the influence of alcohol.

Self-Accessing When Others Make Mistakes

Every time one of our sailors made a mistake, we would assess our own actions to see how we could improve to prevent future mistakes of the same nature by other sailors. Ensuring those making mistakes are accountable for their actions is necessary for their learning and personal growth as well as to prevent others from making similar mistakes. However, it is also important that leaders learn from the experience to improve the opportunities to educate those they lead in preventing future errors. You must be willing to accept that everyone can learn when one team member makes a bad decision. How you approach this can show your people how much you care for them and their success. It is acceptable to show and communicate to your team that they are important to you and to one another. They must know that you want to help them succeed as they help the entire team to succeed.

As previously mentioned, there are various leadership teams on a ship. On an aircraft carrier, there are various areas in which these leadership teams eat and meet to build camaraderie and develop effective communication. The space for my leadership team was the chief petty officer mess. We had over two hundred chief petty officers on USS *George Washington*, and during deployment, there were well over three hundred.

Prior to our deployment, we had welcomed the newly selected chief petty officers onto our leadership team through a process that we at one time called an initiation. This was a four- to six-week process of training. When accomplished properly, it was an effective tool for accepting our new leaders into the leadership team. However, over time, the process became unacceptable in some places. As with every process, it had to be refined to comply with new expectations and practices. Today, we have a new process called CPO 365, which I am proud to have been a part of creating. We support all our first class petty officers throughout the year in developing their leadership skills, and then we welcome them into the chief petty officer mess with a very formal and professional ceremony and what we call a khaki ball. Khaki is the color of the new uniform that all chiefs change into, and the event is also an opportunity to welcome the new spouses onto the team.

Make Sure They Know You Always Care, Even When They Fail

One of the chiefs we welcomed into our chief petty officer mess prior to deployment made a huge mistake. He was caught, by a young group of sailors, kissing a younger sailor in an isolated space. Chief petty officers are not allowed to fraternize with junior sailors. This chief noticed that the sailors had seen him kissing her. He tried to persuade them not to tell anyone what had happened. One of the courageous young sailors knew that this behavior was wrong and told his leaders about it. An investigation was conducted, and the chief was taken to commanding officer's nonjudicial punishment. He was reduced in rank to a second class petty officer, and he was being processed for administrative separation. This resulted in the sailor having to separate from the navy. He had to go home to tell his wife and two kids that he was no longer in the navy. His mistake ended his career and had a devastating impact on his ability to support his family. I spent time with him every day to ensure that he was doing OK, and I told him that although he was no longer a chief petty officer, I wanted him to continue to eat and meet with the others in the chief petty officer mess. I wanted everyone to ensure that he was well before he went home.

Many of the chief petty officers became restless and finally questioned my decision to allow this sailor to come inside the chief petty officer mess. In their eyes, and through his own actions, he was no longer one of us. The situation became extremely contentious, and I had to hold a ship-wide chief's meeting to discuss it. I listened to my teammates' concerns for a few minutes and then started to ask them questions. Who had initiated this sailor to join our CPO mess? How many of them had known that he was struggling with something but not said anything? Had our process of teaching this sailor to be a chief failed in that we did not clearly communicate our expectations to him?

It was easy for the group to point fingers at the individual for having made a mistake, but it was difficult to think that maybe we could have done something differently, as a leadership team, to avoid the whole situation. I then shared with the group that not only had this sailor made a mistake, but he had made an enormous, life-changing mistake, as he was being separated from the navy. I told them that we had the opportunity to help him through this transition and to show him that he had the opportunity to excel outside of the navy. Sending him out of the chief petty officer mess would only isolate him and intensify my concern that he might do something harmful to himself. I did not want to worry about him jumping off the ship in an attempt to end any type of isolation.

Once I convinced them that we had to assess our situation as a leadership team and learn how best to keep it from happening again, they embraced the plan to show the dismissed sailor some compassion. We had the opportunity, as a leadership team, to show him that we still cared for him. Moreover, by conveying our message to the entire group, we were able to let all five thousand sailors know that we cared about them, even if they too made severe errors in judgment. I must share with you that this one mistake, though made by only one member of the team, had us all reflecting on our future behavior and how we needed to look out for each other a great deal more. It made a negative impact to begin with, but in the end, once we had discussed it and worked through it as a group, our leadership team grew even stronger and became a tighter unit.

We do not abandon our people; we support them. They need their leaders most when they make mistakes—for correction and support. This is also a great opportunity for the leaders to evaluate themselves and develop. Challenging events and even failures often generate the most growth. The dismissed sailor did go home, and I kept in touch with him for a long time after that, and he did go on to overcome his mistake. He was able to make amends with his family and find a successful path in life. I credit the incredible leaders in our USS *George Washington* chief petty officer mess for helping him to progress through this difficult time. I was so very proud of how our leadership team had all supported this effort. The situation enabled us to improve in our service to those we led as we learned a great deal through the experience.

Always Work to Promote Your Team

At the same time, we had an outstanding command chaplain on our team. Chaplain Brad Abelson had established a very caring and giving environment that guided us through many ethical and leadership issues. I am sorry to say that we lost Brad a couple of years later to his fight with cancer. He was and continues to be an inspiration to all of us who served with him.

When he departed, we were blessed with another great chaplain, Commander Bob Williams. He also had a passion for helping people. As a matter of fact, he saw an opportunity to develop our young population through a series of life skills training classes. He shared his vision with me and with the executive officer. He and I engaged the first class petty officer leadership team aboard the ship and challenged them to take the lead on teaching the life skills classes that Commander Williams had developed. They took on the challenge and offered the life skills training to our junior sailors. However, Commander Williams wanted to take it to another level. His thought was to have the classes taught primarily to sailors who had been placed on restriction through nonjudicial punishment due to the mistakes they had made. Many times, when sailors are given restriction to the ship, they are also given extra duty for two hours each day. His recommendation was to allow these sailors to attend the series of six classes that focused on various areas. When they successfully completed the classes, they could request a reduction of five days from their sentence. Commander Williams wanted to provide them the motivation to attend while also enabling them to gain the skills that would support their future success. Most importantly, it was an opportunity to once again show our sailors that even if they made a mistake, we still cared about them and wanted them to succeed. Some of these sailors would be separated from the navy, but by investing in them through these classes, we hoped to help them excel in the next chapter of their lives. After all, we still needed them to go forward and become contributing members of society.

Commander Williams put this plan together, and the executive officer scheduled him to present it to our commanding officer, Captain Marty Erdossy. He loved the idea, and so, the process began. Our first class petty officers were given another opportunity to learn from and give back to their sailors. Our many outstanding sailors attended the classes to learn new skills, and our sailors who had made mistakes attended to improve themselves and also reduce the time they would be on restriction. This became another great opportunity to show everyone that we cared about their success. In addition, our caring and giving command climate grew to a new level, and our team once again became stronger.

I use the following statement at the end of my work e-mails as a reminder, not only to others but also to myself: *They do not care how much you know until they know how much you care.* These are more than words; they are actions too. The leaders on USS *George Washington* were all about action and achieving success at every level.

If They Do Not Think You Care about Them, They Will Not Consider You Their Leader

I was very fortunate in my first tour as a command master chief to enter the world of naval aviation. I had spent my first fifteen years in the surface navy and with the Seabees. In the navy, each warfare community has a different culture and way of doing business. I was excited about a new opportunity to learn. I was going to receive my indoctrination to command leadership and naval aviation through Fighter Squadron One Zero Three, the Jolly Rogers. It was an amazing learning experience for me. I had heard many stories of how the command master chief and the maintenance master chief would sometimes get into a power struggle. I sought out many—including my brother-in-law, Master Chief Robert Alley, who was a maintenance master chief—about how to approach developing the command master chief and maintenance master chief relationship so that I would not duplicate the story.

When I reported for duty, I met Master Chief Jimmy Ray, the maintenance master chief. He was a gruff and intimidating character, but it was soon obvious that he truly cared about his sailors and understood the importance of their mission. He made it clear that he had 90 percent of the people in the squadron working for him, and I made it clear that my goal was a partnership that would help the squadron remain on a successful path. I learned a great deal from Jimmy, and together, we worked through issues to ensure that we supported the team. Our friendship continues today thanks to social media. I am grateful that my life has included him. During our time together, we accomplished many great things. We communicated daily and showed our team a unified front. We did not always agree, and there was give-and-take in both directions. Ultimately, our final decisions were based on what was best for the sailors and our mission.

In my first few weeks, my new mentor and the leader I was replacing, Command Master Chief Kevin Daley, was present to help me with the transition. Kevin was promoted to become the Fighter Wing US Atlantic command master chief and remained a mentor of mine for many years. When he departed, I was ready to be a new leader on the team. As I began the tour, young sailors were constantly parading to my office and asking me for help with their current issues. I felt like I was contributing to the solution by helping them become more successful. However, after a couple weeks of this, I realized that I could not get out of my office. The next sailor who came into my office presented me with his issue. I asked him what his chief had told him to do when he had presented the problem to him. The chief was the sailor's senior enlisted leader in his division. He expressed to me that his chief had told him to go see the command master chief, and so, here he was.

I asked the young sailor to go see his chief and tell the chief come to see me.

Please do not take this out of context. The chief is also the technical expert, and he has a very demanding job too. But my job was not to do the chief's job of leading and supporting the sailors at his level. I was now a command level leader and was expected to support and prepare the chiefs in leading our sailors at each level. When the chief came to my office, I asked him what he had told the sailor to do. He expressed that he had told the sailor to go see the command master chief, just as the sailor had expressed. I asked him why he did not help the sailor with his situation, and he stated, "I have jets to fly, Master Chief. I do not have time for that." I told him that those jets of his do not fly without the sailors he leads. This was a mentality that I was promoting in the command, as I was still taking care of their issues. Instead, I should have been showing the chiefs that they were giving their leadership away. They had just become an obstacle to leadership insofar as the sailors had to ask to go see the command master chief.

I went to our maintenance master chief, Jimmy Ray, and shared my concerns with him. He was initially defensive, as he wanted to ensure that his leadership team was first and foremost focused on the mission, but he also understood my point about the chiefs losing the respect of the sailors who needed their leadership. Jimmy and I met with all the chiefs in the squadron and shared my concerns with them. They initially had pushback and tried to create a difference in opinion between Jimmy and me, but we remained unified. I committed to support them and our sailors but only after they had done all that they could for their sailors. If they could not figure out how to assist them, Jimmy and I were both there to offer advice and guidance to support their leadership efforts.

It took some persistence to change the way things operated. But when the chiefs were once again engaged with their sailors, you could see that they had a new level of energy. They had started to notice that their people respected them more because of their actions. Why? Because our sailors could now see that their leaders cared, not only cared about getting the jets to fly but about their personal and professional success. The chiefs were given more authority to deal with their sailors' situations and once again felt like they were leaders on their team. This was a tough lesson for all of us to learn, but we were a stronger group of leaders for having worked through it together, and our sailors could sense that everyone was being given the necessary attention and support.

Be Present with Your Team

In an aviation squadron, as in any military organization, there are layers of leadership teams. In a squadron, this starts with a command leadership team, the ready room of aviator officers, the chief petty officer mess of senior enlisted leaders, and finally the first class petty officer mess of the production level supervisors. After a period of time, I noticed that the aviators would arrive each day, prepare for their flights, and then hang out in the ready room. In the squadron, the aviators are also given leadership responsibilities; they become department heads, division officers, or branch officers. However, this group was not engaged, and the chiefs were taking care of all the responsibilities. This may have explained why our chiefs did not have much time to help our sailors with their various issues. I watched this for a couple of weeks and then spoke to my commanding officer, Commander Craig "Tootsie" Roll. I shared my concerns with him and said that I would like to address the officers at the next all officer meeting. His initial response was, "Are you sure you want to do that?"

My response was, "Are you sure you do not want me to do that? These are your future commanding officers, and I do not want the first time that they engage with and lead sailors to be when they get to that level."

He understood perfectly and had just wanted to ensure that I had a plan to discuss this with the group. So, we conducted the meeting, and I addressed the group. As expected, there was resistance from some, but others understood the importance gaining the support of those they led. The statement I made that truly got their attention was this: "Are you sure you do not want to get to know the sailors that are working on the airplanes you are flying?" I also shared with them that those enlisted sailors would have loved the opportunity to fly had they been given the same opportunity and maybe, in some cases, they could help them achieve their career goals by sharing their personal experience. Yes, they were different from the young officers, and in many cases, the enlisted sailors were older than the officers. But there were great opportunities for interaction that would help the junior personnel reach their goals. And along the way, they may just learn something from the sailors they were leading.

They left the meeting and started the new task. I discussed with CDR Roll how I wanted to cut the space that was the chief petty officer mess in half and turn it into a division and branch office. Doing this would create a space that the branch and division officers could share with the branch and division chiefs who were leading the various divisions. I knew that our officers and chiefs could learn a great deal from each other as well, and in fact, they did. The unity, communication, and understanding across the various leadership teams began to grow, and the respect for leadership was strengthened. Our sailors could see us working together, as a team, at the most senior levels, and they were therefore following our lead. Our overall effectiveness was improving, and this enabled Master Chief Ray and his department head to change the work schedule to a three-shift cycle rather than a two-shift-a-day cycle. Morale was growing, and our people were proud to be a part of the Jolly Rogers.

The overall efforts of every leader on our team had developed, mine included, and the squadron was recognized. Fighter Squadron One Zero Three, the Jolly Rogers, was the very first Tomcat squadron to be awarded the Secretary of Defense Phoenix Award for maintenance excellence. Master Chief Ray had set a new standard, and I felt honored when I was asked to go to Washington, DC, with the group that would be recognized. This was their award, the maintenance department's award, and they asked me to be a part of it. What an amazing honor.

Show Them How They Can Help You Grow

Just as I worked to invest in our sailors, our sailors were investing in me. When you enter a new warfare community as a command master chief in the navy, you are required to qualify in that area. Having never served in the aviation community, this was going to be a significant challenge for me. It would require meeting many qualifications, passing a written test, and then confronting an oral board. I went to our chiefs and asked them for their support in helping me achieve this goal. Each one of them did just that, taking me too many areas and preparing me to learn the jet, processes, and programs. Sometimes I would feel like my head was going to explode, but it was amazing to learn so much about my new community.

I spent time with the young sailors working on the planes to learn what they were doing. You could see how this work energized them. The command master chief was learning something from the nineteen-year-old maintainer! What they did not realize was how much they were energizing me by showing me their passion for their work. They were truly amazing, and I could not have been prouder of our navy for having found such great Americans to serve our country.

At the end of my process, I had passed the written test and was getting ready for my oral board, which would be conducted by some of the senior members of the squadron. CDR Roll came to me and asked if it would be all right if he sat on my board. This was unprecedented, as the commanding officer did not normally sit these boards. Of course, I responded that it was OK. I could not tell him no, but I know he also wanted to ensure that the other sailors who wanted to work toward this qualification knew that it was not simply handed to their command master chief. I had earned it, just as was expected of all members of the team. We conducted the oral board, and over 150 questions were presented to me. Of those, I could not answer only three. CDR Roll was extremely impressed; he asked me, "How did you do that?" He went on to say that he did not think he could have answered all those questions. In one of my proudest moments in that command, I looked at him—along with the various chiefs sitting on the panel—and I said, "Sir, our chiefs got me ready, and they were not going to let me fail. Our sailors taught me the many tasks and gave me their best so that I could give them mine." That moment still makes me tingle all over, and I can still see the big smile of pride on Commander Roll's face. Thank you, shipmates, for the amazing memory. You know who you are.

Inspiring Others to Give Fosters Unity and Success

While the command master chief on USS *George Washington*, we were headed into a one-year maintenance period at the Newport News Shipbuilding. The shipyard is located in the small downtown area of Newport News, and we were about to introduce a new population of sailors to this environment. All aircraft carriers are eventually in this environment, but due to rotation of personnel, there is always a new population moving off the ship and living in the local area. This presented many new challenges since many would be living in town on their own for the first time with new levels of responsibility on a personal level. Oftentimes when a new ship was in Newport News, the city would take a beating because of issues associated with sailors not taking care of the local area or creating mischief with the local population.

The executive officer, Captain Dee Mewbourne, our chaplain, Commander Bob Williams, and I all knew we had to do something different for our crew. Captain Mewbourne's idea was to focus on giving back to the community versus just letting our sailors make up their minds how they would treat the new environment. We would show them that serving their community was just as important as serving our nation. The chaplain was responsible for the community service program and presented the idea that over the one-year period, we would commit to completing two thousand hours of community service. Captain Mewbourne looked a little confused when presented with the two thousand hours. He stated that we had more than two thousand sailors on board and that surely we could ensure each sailor gave more than one hour. He said we needed to create a big, hairy, audacious goal and then insisted that we should be able to achieve twenty thousand hours. The chaplain first looked overwhelmed at the thought that we could do this much. He then realized that this goal was not going away and stated that it would take tremendous command support. Captain Mewbourne told him he had it, and the planning began.

Prior to arrival in the shipyard, Chaplain Williams had established contact with the Newport News mayor's office and worked with his community service coordinator. Our first day entering the shipyard dry dock required a large population of the crew to be off the ship. This became the opportunity to introduce the crew to Newport News in a positive manner. Those who were not on the ship for the dry dock would be across Newport News, serving. Each department was given a location and a project in parks, shelters, or beautification areas. In that one day, our crew delivered eight hundred hours of community service in Newport News.

Mayor Frank had been the mayor of Newport News for many years, and he had never seen anything like this. I drove around the city with him to visit the various locations at which our sailors were serving, and he was thanking them almost with tears in his eyes. Our sailors could truly see his appreciation. Many of the projects could not be completed in the time frame that we had that day. The next week, I learned that our crew did not like unfinished business, as many of the departments were now going back to their locations at the end of their workdays to complete projects and start new ones. They had established relationships with the many nonprofit organizations and wanted to continue to support their efforts.

Also prior to our arrival in the shipyard, we had the police department brief our crew on areas of high crime and where they had previously seen sailors getting into trouble. Our sailors responded by giving back and staying away from problem areas.

Captain Mewbourne and I departed during the shipyard period, and the new commanding officer, Captain Garry White, continued to support the program. At the end of the shipyard period, the police department came back and bragged about how our crew had the lowest rate of incidents associated with sailors in town compared to any other aircraft carrier. The USS *George Washington* had contributed over 22,000 hours of community service in supporting Newport News. Mayor Frank and his city were so grateful that they hosted a thank-you picnic for the crew on the ship. They presented the crew with a large-screen television that could be placed on the mess decks to support their morale program, as they had had a significant impact on the morale of the people living in Newport News.

The impact was huge, and we, once again, were able to show our crew that we cared about their success. Probably more importantly, they saw that they could contribute to the success of others through their own actions. Captain Mewbourne's big, hairy, audacious goal was a huge success for our team, and we all learned a great deal from the experience.

Staying Focused on Caring for and Developing Others

An organization is reflective of its leaders at the top. As the command master chief, I was the senior enlisted leader. In these various commands, the enlisted force is the largest population. It was important for me to not only ensure that our entire team heard the expectations but also display the conduct and execution of responsibilities that I wanted them to emulate. To accomplish this, I came up with three questions that I would present to myself on a daily basis to ensure that I completed my own self-reflection. Those three questions are as follows:

1. Did I wake up with a positive attitude and with the motivation of developing a positive environment for those around me?
2. Did I begin my day with the goal of helping those around me to grow and succeed?
3. `Did I do all that I could to give my very best to those I serve as a leader?

Your reflection should not be a weekly check but one that is made throughout each day. Your influence is, first and foremost, a visual image you project to those you lead. If you expect others to perform at a certain level, you must first ask yourself if you, as their leader, are performing at a higher level. If you only communicate these expectations and then sit back and watch while everyone works to meet them, you may want to ask yourself, "What expectations are they working to emulate? The ones you are speaking of or the ones you are modeling?"

If you are a giving and caring person, those around you will recognize that this has contributed to your success. Your success will be desired by others around you and they will therefore work to copy your success. Once again, are you happy with the example you are asking them to emulate? Giving back to others is, in my experience, the most gratifying thing you can do for yourself. Now, just imagine what it will feel like when others start to emulate your behavior. Your leadership example will grow forward as they work to replicate your success. They do not care how much you know until they know how much you care.

POP Points

- It is acceptable to show and communicate to your team that they are important to you.
- It is when teammates make a mistake that they need their leader the most. How you respond to them may dictate whether they still consider you their leader.
- The most challenging times are often the times in which we learn the most.
- As communication, understanding, and unity increase, the respect and strength of the leadership team also increases.
- As you invest in those you lead, they will invest in you.
- They do not care how much you know until they know how much you care.

Recommended reading: *Good to Great,* by Jim Collins.

CHAPTER 10

(L3+CE)
Leadership Is Not a Mathematical Equation, or Is It?

THIS CHAPTER IS dedicated to my good friend and mentor, the twelfth master chief petty officer of the navy, Rick West. He is a true friend and shipmate, and he sets a shining example for all leaders to follow.

In these next three chapters, I will discuss the leadership concepts that I have developed to communicate to others those ideas that focus on positive leadership. As a leader, how you communicate to various audiences will determine your success. Know your audience and what is most important to them, and then work to connect with them. As we previously discussed, Abraham Lincoln's success in this area allowed the masses to both understand him and grasp that he actually understood them too. This gift is what eventually won him the presidency.

John Maxwell's book, *Everyone Communicates, Few Connect,* focuses on this topic as well. It is a great read, and it will help you understand the importance of effective communication at all levels. What follow below are a few points that I have used with general audiences that I hope you will find useful in developing your own messages to communicate the Power of Positive Leadership.

As I previously shared with you, Chief of Naval Operations Admiral Mullen would often use this motto so that his leaders would understand the importance of servant leadership: "Listen, learn, and lead." I feel confident that he was not the first to come up with this concept, but it was still a great message for him to share with others.

A recent chief of naval operations used the same words to describe a very good friend of mine, Rick West. Rick was the twelfth master chief petty officer of the navy (MCPON). He was our navy's most senior enlisted leader, who advised the chief of naval operations on all matters associated with enlisted personnel. As I reflected on what the chief of naval operations had said about my friend, and the leader of the enlisted force in the US Navy, I was inspired to create an equation, since I felt that his description fell short of portraying the man I truly admired. Although leadership is not really a mathematical equation, reflecting on the qualities of our MCPON led me to compile the most necessary aspects of leadership into something that looks like one.

Rick West was and still is great in all three areas. But as I watched and learned from him, I felt that two other principles would also help others to understand the importance of leadership. Every successful leader must be an effective communicator and educator. During his time as the MCPON, Rick viewed his position as one in which he could definitely listen, learn, and lead. I watched him use this platform to communicate his expectations around the world and then educate others on the changes that had been implemented due to his listening and learning. This is how I came to develop the equation (L3+CE), as the principles of leadership must include *communication* and *education*.

To complement MCPON West's efforts, as fleet master chief of manpower, personnel, training, and education, I created a program called Sailor Grams in which I would formulate a monthly leadership document for distribution across our navy. The following is how (L3+CE) was explained in one such document:

Listen (L1): All good leaders must be willing to listen to those they lead, as well as other influencers, to make good decisions. If you fail to listen, you will most likely not be seen as a leader but as a dictator. Listening to and understanding the needs and resources of those you serve enables you to lead them effectively.

Learn (L2): All good leaders must also be willing to learn. They must develop themselves on a continuous basis, both personally and professionally, if they expect to lead a team to great success. When a leader fails to learn, they fail to grow, and therefore the team never grows. At the same time, a leader must be willing to learn from those they serve and work to understand the challenges so that they can assist in improving the outcomes of various situation.

Lead (L3): Once you start to listen and learn, only then can you lead and effect positive change. A good leader must influence others with useful information and resources that will lead them to success.

Now that the three *L*s have been defined, you must continue on to the *C* and *E*:

Communicate (C): Communication is essential for any effective leader. Once you start to listen to and learn from those around you, you must continue to lead. Now, return to your team and communicate your expectations and support.

Educate (E): Education is critical as you communicate. To promote success, you must be able to learn from your actions and teach those lessons to the ones you are leading. As the team starts to understand the challenges you take on and the decisions that you make, they will need to become smarter so that they can support those challenges and decisions. Thus, they may also be able to assist you with innovations so that you can all achieve your goals.

Always Work to Improve Communication

Communicating the principles of leadership may appear to be easy, but if it were easy, everyone would be a successful leader. And this is not the case. With leading, a great deal of learning occurs through making mistakes. One of the easiest ways to make a mistake is to take for granted that you are sufficiently communicating to and educating those you lead. I believe that you could walk into any organization, and the one way in which you could immediately improve that organization is through increasing their communication.

We are in a dynamic and ever-changing world of technology, filled with tools that our current and future workforce are using to communicate. On a leadership level, failure to continue learning about these tools and how they are being utilized can lead to disaster. The leader of a team cannot fail to understand their means of communication. If you do not communicate with your team in a way they are willing to accept, you are falling short of your leadership potential and may just lose your competitive edge.

Listening and learning are self-explanatory and require effort. However, leading requires a great deal more than just these two activities. I hope I have continued to show you this through many of the examples. Adding to the leadership equation "CE" can help others understand the importance that effective communication and education play in becoming a stronger leader.

Frequent Positive Focused Communications

Your communications are extremely important and must have a positive tone. There may be times when a negative means of communication is necessary, but these should be limited. Moreover, such exchanges must be held privately as often as possible so that you do not embarrass yourself or the person or group receiving the negative message. How you communicate will in part determine the type of leader you are or become. Your positive messages and overall projection will leave a lasting impression on the masses, who will then want to emulate you.

Find Your "Hooyah"

During his time as MCPON, Rick West was always a motivating force. He coined the term "hooyah," which our sailors continue to use today as a source of motivation. I can still picture him in front of large groups of sailors, screaming at the top of his lungs, working the crowd up to be proud of their service and want to give their very best to the navy. He would finish with leading the entire crowd in screaming this word, loud and proud: "Hooyah!" He still uses this term today, in retirement, and still motivates sailors around the world as he continues to serve them.

As I reviewed my thoughts on this section, I thought about one of the most prevalent retail stores in our country. When they first began to grow, they focused on customer service. This was partly inspired by a daily shift meeting, in the middle of the store, in which they would chant to motivate themselves. Doing so brought them together as a team and made them feel that they were contributing to the growth and overall success of the organization. If I were to name this organization and ask you to tell me how they are doing today, I bet you would complain about their level of customer service and their perceived lack of positive motivation in the workplace. The team lost sight of the basics because their leaders lost focus on the importance of keeping them invested in their work. Years ago, it was not about the wages; it was about being a part of a successful team who inspired teamwork. They knew that they were a part of something bigger than themselves.

MCPON West had a knack for ensuring that his sailors knew how important they were with one simple "boost word." This word may have also been effective on a little league sports team. In fact, each service has their own word or expression of pride, and as each service member proudly expresses theirs, they feel a stronger sense of belonging. I can assure you that our young service members are not overpaid, but they are damned proud to serve their country and thus be a part of something bigger than themselves. These expressions remind them of that each and every day.

It is my hope that you learn something from this that will enable you to promote the message of positive energy and project how this message can motivate others. Consider how you, as a leader, communicate with your team and always find a way to include a "hooyah" moment. They will be proud of what they do, and so, they will be energized when they face the next challenge on their path to success.

Exercising POP

When I first kicked off my efforts to communicate POP Leadership throughout the navy, I presented the idea to my boss, Rear Admiral Boensel. He supported my efforts, and we sent out a region-wide message, to all commands in our seventeen states, to express two proposals. The first was making me available to present the Power of Positive Leadership to those who wanted to focus on leadership with their team. The second was creating a process whereby positive reinforcement would be promoted.

Over time, people would complain about our young sailors not doing something correctly, such as wearing their uniforms. Attention to detail is important in the military, and wearing the uniform properly reinforces this point each time you prepare for your workday. As leaders continued to complain about their sailors' noncompliance, I would ask them, "How many did you notice who were wearing their uniforms properly?" Sometimes, you have to point out the need for a change in perspective. Of course, we had placed so much focus on pointing out errors that we often failed to take the time to recognize those who were wearing their uniforms properly.

The process I created and presented in my message to all commands in those seventeen states was simple. As a leader, if you identified a sailor from another command not following a rule, such as wearing his or her uniform incorrectly, you were to discover the name and command of that sailor and note them with the discrepancy. You would then send an e-mail containing this information to me, and I would pass it along to the appropriate leader in the sailor's command. This would ensure that the issue was addressed and resolved. However, for each negative discrepancy they sent me, these leaders had to also send me two positive interactions they had had with sailors for doing something well.

We promoted this process for six months, and in those six months, I received one particular e-mail from two first class petty officers on shore patrol. They had seen a young sailor, Aviation Boatswain Mate Fuels Third Class (ABF3) Washington, from USS *George Washington*, while he had been pumping gas in his car. They had approached him, and as they had, you can imagine the concern he must have felt from seeing two shore patrol officers. He had been in his service dress blue uniform—or crackerjacks, as some call them—and he had looked sharp. They had stated, "Shipmate, you look sharp in your uniform, and we just wanted to thank you for representing our navy team like this." They had sent me the e-mail the following morning, sharing how this young third class petty officer had lit up when they had recognized him for his efforts. I in turn sent this e-mail to the command master chief of USS *George Washington*, who shared it with the sailor's department head, department leading chief, executive officer, and commanding officer.

The next day, the division chief called ABF3 Washington up in front of everyone at the morning muster; he discussed the incident with him and thanked him for setting a positive example. He then told ABF3 Washington to take the rest of the day off. Can you imagine what his peers were thinking?

The following morning, the commanding officer got on the ship's announcement system and called ABF3 Washington to his in-port cabin. He thanked ABF3 Washington, gave him a personal challenge coin, and then took him down to the ship's announcement system. A challenge coin is a token of appreciation that many leaders throughout the military hand out. It is generally slightly larger than a half-dollar, has the command logo on one side, and, on the other side, includes something about the leader that is presenting the coin, to include their name. They are called challenge coins because if you are challenged with a similar coin while in a drinking establishment and do not have yours on you, you are expected to buy the person who challenged you a drink. If that person challenges you and you do have the coin, the challenger has to buy you a drink. After giving the coin to ABF3 Washington, the commanding officer communicated what had happened to the entire crew, and applauded the great example that one sailor had provided by representing his shipmates well, even while on liberty. The command master chief called me the next day and expressed what an impact this one action had had on his entire crew. One simple statement of recognition had turned into a lesson on the importance of acknowledging excellence, and it reinforced what you can expect to happen when you do the right thing.

I share all of this with you to, once again, talk about my good friend Rick West. While all of this was going on, he was the US Fleet Forces fleet master chief, and he supported my efforts. I will never forget this one time at our submarine base in Groton, Connecticut. I was having dinner with Force Master Chief Kevin Blade, who was traveling with me to my installations. Kevin is a great leader, and he wanted to reinforce to his region command master chiefs the importance of their being out and about so that they could learn of the sailors' challenges. Kevin led by example and always with a focus on those we served. While we were having dinner at the famous Mystic Pizza in Mystic, Connecticut, my cell phone started to ring. I answered it, and—to my surprise—someone said, "Well, hello, shipmate." Yes, it was Fleet Master Chief Rick West. At the time, I was thinking, *This cannot be good. He is calling me in the evening.* But then he said, "You are not going to believe this. That **POP** stuff really works." He had my attention now!

He shared that he had stopped three sharp-looking sailors and complimented them on their uniforms. He had given them his business card and told them to take it back to their ship and have their command master chief give him a call. Of course, they had done so. Rick stated that before he could get back to his office, the command master chief had left a voice mail. He had returned the call, and they had had a conversation about how this one simple moment of recognition had sparked excitement in his entire crew because one of their own was being recognized by the fleet master chief. It had also enabled them to understand the impact of a positive interaction. They had gotten their "hooyah" moment thanks to one simple act of kindness.

I am still not sure whether Rick knows how much he did for me through that phone call, simply by expressing that he had recognized my efforts and was now reinforcing them himself, adjusting his own approach to teach others. Once again, he had created a "hooyah" moment—and, yes, MCPON West, this POP stuff really works! "Hooyah," Master Chief Petty Officer of the Navy Rick West! "Hooyah," shipmates!

Do you have your daily "hooyah" moment with your team?

POP Points

- Listen.
- Learn.
- Lead.
- Communicate.
- Educate.
- How you communicate determines how you project yourself as a leader.
- "Hooyah!"

Recommended reading: *Everyone Communicates, Few Connect*, by John C. Maxwell.

CHAPTER 11

T+I+E:
How Do You Tie This All Together to Grow?

THINK ABOUT THE need to tie your shoelaces—the importance of bringing two sides together to hold a very important tool on your foot for protection from the various environments you will travel. Can there be a simpler comparison to the importance of bringing teams together to accomplish a mission? You have an opening in your shoe, and you have two sides that are naturally pulling away from each other. So, you put this simple lace through the various loops and you pull it tightly; then you tie a knot to keep the two sides together to ensure the mission of safety for your foot. Picture yourself as the lace. Do you bring teams together and build teamwork to enable their success?

In each branch of military service, as with any company, there are many subcultures that ultimately work together, through their various leaders, to complete an overall mission. As our thirtieth chief of naval operations (CNO), Admiral Jonathon Greenert, assumed his role, he worked diligently to bring his team together through his first message to the navy. He intentionally did not speak to any one specific group but to all who served on his team. He stated, "I am honored to be your chief of naval operations. Drawing upon two centuries of heritage and tradition, I trust that, when called upon, you will perform superbly. You exemplify the highest standards of service to our nation."

In making this statement, CNO Greenert encompasses many positive leadership traits. His words express how humbled he was by the opportunity he had been given. The trust he had developed with those on his team was the reason for that opportunity. He continued to seek the trust of those he led and supported, and he worked to influence all of them to inspire success. His many years of experience on top of the trust he had earned enabled all those who served to accept his influence. How do you define leadership, and how do you tie it all together?

Using Rejection to Motivate Growth

I will share with you that I interviewed twice with Admiral Greenert, for two separate positions, to serve as his fleet master chief and as his master chief petty officer of the navy. In both cases, he selected someone else, and they were both outstanding leaders and friends. This in no way diminishes my perception of his leadership of our navy team, as he was very successful in the role. After selecting my good friend Fleet Master Chief Tom Howard, he did support me in my application for the fleet master chief of manpower, personnel, training, and education position, and I was selected. He did what he felt was best at the time, for his sailors and his approach to leadership, and I had to respect his perspective and grow from the experience.

Never lose sight of your goals, and never let anyone slow your progress or prevent you from an opportunity to learn and grow. In many ways, Admiral Greenert's decision to not choose me only made me more determined to improve. Life is not about winning or losing in a selection processes; it is about serving and doing your very best to ensure that those you support get the information they need to make good decisions. Admiral Greenert assisted me, through his actions, in reaching these goals, and I am grateful for it as I was therefore able to work at the highest levels of leadership to bring teams together. I was afforded the opportunity at my various professional levels of leadership to be "the lace" that brings teams together by breaking down community barriers.

In doing so, I learned the importance of TIE Leadership. And this became the important topic of another sailor gram, whose message was simple. Hopefully this offers you another easy acronym to recall during the execution and communication of your leadership responsibilities.

(T+I+E) = Leadership

Trust: Merriam-*Webster's Dictionary* defines trust as "assured reliance on the character, ability, strength, or truth of someone or something." Think about this. Would you follow a leader who did not encompass this definition? Developing trust with those you lead will enable you to have stronger influence. How do you work to develop trust with those you are serving at all levels?

Influence: Merriam-Webster's defines Influence as "the act or power of producing an effect without apparent exertion of force or direct exercise of command." In other words, it is the act of accomplishing things through those you lead and serve. As you develop trust with your good example, your team will become more willing to listen to and learn from you. They do this based on the way you live your life and what you can offer to help them improve.

Experience: Experience is more than holding a position a period of time. It is the active learning that you exercise during the execution of your responsibilities and how you apply the knowledge you obtain to future tasks. The more experience you have, the more you have learned, and this prepares you not only to develop yourself but also to share with others as you lead them to develop too. Do you share your experience with others to build trust and influence?

Always remember that many leaders may be given the opportunity to lead, but a team will follow a leader only if they choose to. Great leaders are not served by those they lead; great leaders serve those they lead and "TIE" it all together to accomplish the mission at hand. Admiral Greenert led by example—how are you working on TIE with your team? The example you set as a leader can have a very positive impact on those who lead within your organization. They may become a positive influence multiplier for all those you lead and serve. No matter where you are in the organization, you are a leader, and you must work to build on these traits for the team's success.

Remove Barriers and Build Bridges

Think about any organization that you have been a part of. Within the organization, many teams are working to accomplish smaller missions or objectives with the goal of securing success for the entire team. You can even apply this to your family unit: everyone may have different aspirations and may be pulling you in different directions, but when you all work together, you obtain the knowledge you need to secure the success of everyone involved. To break down invisible barriers across the many teams, you must build trust. Once you develop trust, and once they see that you are invested in their success and how important it is to the overall success of the team, you can then begin to influence them and share your experience on how to better achieve success.

Think about a football team. There are many leaders on the team whose mission is to win the game. But there are also many teams working in various positions to secure success for the entire team. The quarterback is often viewed as the team leader of the players. Although he may officially be the leader of the offense, he must develop relationships with the defensive and special teams too, to show them how important their contributions are to winning the game. You cannot score points if you never get the football, and the only way to get the football is for your smaller teams to perform at full potential. Great quarterbacks secure success for their team because they are willing to consider all aspects of the game and learn how to better contribute to the smaller team's success. When everyone in those various positions sees that they are valued, they tend to work harder to reach their team's goal.

I am not a New England Patriots fan, but you have to admire the success that they have achieved over the past two decades. I am not a Tom Brady fan either—and there have been many discussions on whether this team plays fairly—but you have to again admire how this team sticks together through thick and thin, always supporting each other. This culture is ultimately determined by their head coach Bill Belichick, but his demands are replicated by the many leaders on the team. They focus on getting better every day, and they all work to inspire each other to reach new levels of success. If you do not buy into the culture, coaches are not afraid to let you go. Many players have played for them, and many of those players have moved on.

This team breaks down barriers, and they understand the importance of contributing to all parts of the team by building bridges of support. They appreciate that they are not successful without each one of them, and therefore, the trust they have for one another is higher than that of most professional football teams. As they have developed that trust, they have also learned how to communicate with each other in a respectful manner and share their experience, thus influencing greater performance across the entire team.

Building Bridges Leads to Unity and Success

I have already shared the story of breaking down a barrier between the chief petty officers and the first class petty officers and how, together, we improved the contribution and effectiveness of our first class petty officer leadership team on USS George Washington. Another situation that may have been even more difficult to achieve was breaking down the barriers between the senior enlisted in the chief petty officer mess and the officers in the wardroom. Of course, we had our many different roles in the leadership group; however, we would learn that we all had the same objective: to serve those we lead and successfully complete our mission.

After being on board for a period of time, and as we were getting ready for our deployment, I noticed that the relationships between our officers and our senior enlisted were not as strong as they could or should have been. I tried to figure out how I was going to overcome this. The chief petty officer mess and the wardroom locations are both restricted to only leaders who are in their respective leadership group. Officers did not go into the chief petty officer mess unless invited, and chiefs did not go into the wardroom unless invited. There were times when I would invite the captain or the executive officer into the chief petty officer mess for a meal and to spend time with the chiefs. The executive officer would occasionally invite me into the wardroom for a meal, and the captain would sometimes invite me and the executive officer to his dining room. This was important for our communications but it also showed the other leaders on the team that we were working together and unified in our efforts. This was an important visual, and we needed to somehow replicate this situation at all levels with the senior enlisted and officers.

As we began our deployment, I thought about how we could get everyone together. Both spaces were too small to have everyone together for a meal, but I thought maybe we could invite the officers into the chief petty officer mess for what we called an ice cream social. I went to our executive officer, Captain Dee Mewbourne, and presented the idea to him, and he loved it. We would take one evening and, after the dinner meal, have an ice cream social in the chief petty officer mess. At the next chief petty officer training meeting, I presented the idea to the group. I did not expect that a group of chiefs would be upset by my allowing officers into the chief petty officer mess. We had a lively discussion: first, I listened to their concerns, and then I expressed my own concerns about the lack of communication that existed between the two groups. Some of them were still not happy with the idea. I rarely ever did this, but as the leader of the chief petty officer mess, I expressed that this was one time that I would have 51 percent of the vote, so this was going to happen. Conflict is good, and this discussion was actually an opportunity to learn about our own reservations over working with another group of leaders. As the group of outstanding chief petty officers always did on our ship, they supported my efforts going forward.

As we promoted the idea among the two groups, the excitement started to build. The officers were all very excited for the opportunity to come into the chief petty officer mess. Our first run at this was just to have some ice cream—with all the toppings desired—and enjoy each other's company. As I left my office and headed toward the chief petty officer mess, about thirty minutes prior to the event to ensure that we were ready, I could not believe what I was seeing. There was a line of officers from the entrance to the chief petty officer mess to the other end of the ship. Keep in mind that the aircraft carrier is a very long ship. I thought, *we are never going to get everyone in there.*

As the evening progressed, everyone recognized the space constraints and expanded into the wardroom. It was amazing to see people spending time together and having regular conversations just to get to know each other. I was extremely proud of all our chief petty officers. What I had not expected, however, was the feedback I was getting from the same chiefs who had been against having this event in the first place. A few of them came to me and thanked me, stating how rewarding it had been. A couple even expressed that they were now talking to officers in their department who they had never talked to before. As they said this, I thought, *How does this happen?* The ice cream social was a huge success, and the executive officer and I judged it a tremendous win in fostering teamwork and communication.

Sometimes when you do things like this, you never really expect the secondary effects. During our next month of deployment, the officers invited the chief petty officers for an ice cream social in the wardroom. We all attended, and in addition to ice cream, they had candy and decks of cards on the tables to encourage longer engagements. What we did not realize was that, in the background of all of this, was the food service staff for both locations working together to enable the best possible event for the leadership teams. They too had turned this into an opportunity to help each other, and with each event, they raised the bar on what those events would look like. In turns, we held this event monthly for the duration of the six-month deployment.

During the next ice cream social in the chief petty officer mess, we were in the middle of our Navy and Marine Corps Relief Society Fund Drive, which helps sailors (and their families) who are struggling with financial issues. The fund drive is an annual event. I stated that I would greet everyone at the door for the ice cream social, but if they were not in the same uniform that I was, they would have to give a one-dollar donation to get in. This generated a new level of excitement. People would try to get me to tell them what uniform I would be wearing. We were underway, and we all wear a working underway uniform. However, I took my uniform to the chief petty officer mess in a garment bag and then greeted the officers in my dinner dress uniform, which is equivalent to a tuxedo. Of course, everyone had to provide a one-dollar donation to get in. What I had not expected was that, because we were doing this to support our sailors, many were giving much more than one dollar. Some were giving checks for twenty-five dollars through one hundred dollars just to show their appreciation for our using this event to show support for our sailors. In this one event, we raised over $1,000 to contribute to the Navy and Marine Corp Relief Society. Not only were we increasing communication across the team, but we were also showing those we served in our leadership role that we truly cared about them. At the next ship-wide telecast the executive officer and I, on behalf of the wardroom and chief petty officer mess, presented the check to show our sailors that we were supporting them together through the fund drive. What a great thing it was for our crew to see unity within the two groups.

The final event was meant to be held in the wardroom. I went to Captain Mewbourne and said that we would like to have the last one in the chief petty officer mess, where this had all started. The food service teams from the two locations came together and made recommendations of what they would like to do together to make this event special. I was absolutely amazed by what they put together. There we were, in the middle of the ocean, on a war ship. They took this industrial-looking dining area and draped sheets from the overhead to cover the pipes that ran through the space to make the lights appear dimmed. They then created fourteen dessert bars that offered cakes, pies, ice cream, and just about any other dessert you could think of. The food was displayed as if we were in a five-star restaurant. In one corner of the space, a band was set up to play music. What was most impressive about the band was that it comprised both officers and chief petty officers. They had been practicing for the event together so that they could add a new level of class and entertainment to the event. I have to tell you that this all brought tears to my eyes.

Feeling Pride When You TIE It All Together

As I look back on my navy career, I realize that I have spent many years breaking down barriers between groups of leaders to increase their effectiveness and unity. Being a fleet master chief in the US Navy was a tremendous and humbling honor. But my best tour in the navy was as the command master chief of USS *George Washington*. This is not due to anything that I accomplished. Rather, this is due to the amazing people who I was so fortunate to serve with on this crew. From the most senior sailor in Captain Martin Erdossy III to the most junior sailor, scrubbing the pots in the scullery, they were all amazing. Their commitment to serving our nation and each other is something that I will never forget, and I am grateful to have been a small part of our overall success.

Break down those barriers and build bridges. Show people that you can come together to achieve a common goal through a well-communicated message that initiates understanding how the Power of Positive leadership can impact those you lead. You will grow success at a level you have never experienced. Breaking down barriers enables you to TIE everything together. My fellow sailors and I all gained a great deal of experience from our time together, as we developed a tremendous amount of trust and influence and grew together as a team to complete our mission.

Take a look at your organization. Are there places where relationships are weak and need work? Can you break down some of the barriers and begin to rebuild the trust so that you, with the experience you have gained, can begin to influence success for the entire team? How do you TIE this all together and lead them to even greater success? I know, again with the questions. But we all need to contemplate these questions if we are going to dig deep and become stronger leaders by identifying our own weaknesses as well as those across our teams. Failing to do this will eventually create a culture of failure, and I know that absolutely no one wants that. Seek success through the many opportunities you get to improve your team by closing the gaps, and you will achieve a positive culture. You are the one—the one leader—who can make this happen for your team.

POP Points

- Trust.
- Influence.
- Experience.
- No matter where you are in your organization, you are a leader, and you must work to build on these traits for your team's success.
- To break down invisible barriers across the many teams in an organization, you must build trust.
- Break down barriers and build bridges.

CHAPTER 12

ICE:
Sometimes You Just Need to Chill Out! (CSADD)

I GUESS WHAT they say is true, about how you often save your best for last, or in this case, my favorite for last. This chapter may just be my favorite one to share with you, as I get to talk about the amazing young people who serve our country in the US Navy.

Valuing Our Youth

People often say that young people today are not as good as they used to be. I think that many who make this statement have a jealous streak, as they fear that their generation may no longer be seen as the greatest generation, no matter what age group they fall into. Let us first try not to stereotype anyone, and while I brag about the small percentage of Americans who make the commitment to serve their country, know that I believe our youth, throughout the nation, are absolutely amazing and maybe even better than we were at their age. This, of course, is because previous generations were inspired to make the world a better place for the following generations, and each has been successful in doing so. While our world is always a work in progress, our young people today are more informed and better prepared owing to the capabilities that have been created for them by those of us who came before them. I hope that this young generation will one day look back at an even younger one and say, "Look how smart this new generation is." And why will they be smart? Because the previous generation prepared them for success.

This ramble may serve only to stress my personal view of how smart and motivated our young people are; however, I do believe that people need to think about what they are saying and how they are contributing to making others stronger and our world better for those we will one day have left behind.

Developing Peer Mentoring (CSADD)

ICE was a concept that I developed back in 2008, while I was the command master chief at Navy Region Mid-Atlantic. As I have previously mentioned, Rear Admiral Mark Boensel was my boss at the time, and we would routinely talk about how we could provide the very best for those we served and how we could also include sailors, civilians, and family members. At the beginning of the year, we experienced an increase in driving-under-the-influence violations across the seventeen states we served and led. It was becoming very difficult to figure out how to get this behavior under control. The majority of these violations affected our young sailors in the age group of eighteen to twenty-five. It was tough to see this group of young people, who had made the amazing commitment to serve their country, struggle through this type of failure. Many campaigns had been held across our organization to address and raise awareness about the issue, such as a Right Spirit Campaign and other training evolutions. Sometimes it seemed like the more you discouraged your sailors from engaging in this behavior, the more they did just that.

We knew we needed to do something different, so we discussed how this group differed from other groups of leaders on our navy team. Their age and maturity were obvious factors, and both had been previously considered in addressing our concerns. As we looked at the more-senior-in-age groups, we realized that we had the more-senior-in-rank groups too—and the more senior you got, the more likely you were to be a part of a leadership peer group. The group of eighteen-to-twenty-five-year-olds includes mostly the E-1 to E-5 pay grades. Once you made pay grade E-6, you were likely out of the age group most at risk of facing drinking-related issues. They did occur in other age groups, of course, but this was where most offenses occurred.

Once you made E-6, you were called a first class petty officer. As a first class petty officer, you could join the first class petty officer mess. Once you were in pay grades E-7 through E-9, you were called a chief, senior chief, or master chief petty officer, and you were a member of the chief petty officer mess. As an officer, you were a member of the ward-room. And so, you were not really a leader until you reached E-6 and not a member of a leadership team until you reached the same level.

As I have mentioned many times throughout this book, I have always believed that every member of the team is a leader. However, this young group of sailors did not see themselves that way. We were all a member of our great navy team, but this young group of sailors did not feel as connected to the team as the other groups of leaders did. I called this a lack of "service connectedness." Oftentimes, leaders would stereotype this young group, due to the surplus of violations they incurred, and have them all feeling like they were the problem instead of recogniz-ing that they had the greatest opportunity to be a part of the solution. How could we use the Power of Positive Leadership to turn this behavior around and have our young leaders understand their importance? How could we learn from them? How could we secure success for their peer group? And, better yet, how could they enable their peer group to be successful?

We had exhausted ourselves by thinking that they would listen to us solely because we were senior. Do you ever recall what it was like to hear your mom and dad tell you *I told you so?* Our sailors were no different in that they did not want to be treated like little kids. They wanted to be treated like adults, as they were no different than the rest of us insofar as they had also made the remarkable commitment to serve their country through service in the navy. My thought was, *How can we make them part of the solution in securing success and stop seeing them as the problem?* I needed to try a new tactic that was similar to what the other leadership peer groups had developed. This was service connectedness, or being a part of a leadership team. We needed to enable our sailors to demonstrate that they could lead success and not become a part of a failed effort. I then pondered, *What is the most effective team in our nation to address drunk driving?* Of course, I thought of Mothers Against Drunk Driving (MADD). I knew that I could not create a group myself. If this was going to be successful, our young sailors had to create something special for their peers. Rear Admiral Boensel agreed with my approach, and he enabled me to move forward.

I pitched the concept to the small group of sailors in the appropriate age group and asked them to explore the idea of Sailors Against Drunk Driving (SADD). I shared with them that this would be their opportunity to have a positive impact on their peer group. I also shared the MADD model with them and then sent them on their way to start holding meetings to discuss what they would design. It was my intent to inspire them to create something that would be enduring and show everyone that our junior sailors were not the problem but rather the solution to resolving the issue of drunk driving.

I assigned Chief Petty Officer David Rivette to support the group— not to lead it but to be present to assist them with obtaining the necessary materials and resources to facilitate their creation. After attending many meetings and discussions, Chief Rivette returned to me and stated that he just sat in the back of the room and let the young sailors discuss the issue, and that they were going to blow me away with their thought process.

The four sailors in the age group of eighteen to twenty-five—MC2 Timothy Comerford, GM2 Erica Pearson, GSM2 Benjamin Daley, and QM2 Timothy Wright—came into my office and shared that they had spent many meetings discussing their ideas with other shipmates. They had looked at using Sailors Against Drunk Driving (SADD), but that acronym was already used by Students Against Drunk Driving. They also shared that they thought driving under the influence began with a bad decision, and they felt that they could address more than just drunk driving by addressing the larger decision-making process. They felt that if they could address the importance of making better decisions, they would reduce drunk driving as well as other destructive choices. They stated that they wanted their group to be called the Coalition of Sailors Against Destructive Decisions (CSADD). Chief Rivette had been right; they blew me away. I had them present their idea to our Navy Region Mid-Atlantic commander, RADM Boensel. He strongly supported the idea, and so, in January 2008, the founding chapter of CSADD was established at Navy Region Mid-Atlantic.

Never underestimate the power and impact of a small group of people willing to make a positive change for all. Not only was I able to inspire their actions in creating this group, but they also inspired me with their focus and determination.

At this point, I began to challenge the group to develop visual aids, training programs, and advertisements for the program. The first challenge was for the group to establish a campaign to promote the program. The campaign title they created was *Stop and Think*. The sailors' thought process was that if each person would stop for three seconds prior to acting to think of the outcome, they could make a very impactful difference on that outcome. I then challenged them to create a visual training program that involved everyone in the audience versus only a PowerPoint presentation. These young leaders created a DUI scenario for the group of sailors to perform onstage. Every member of the audience was a family member to one of the actors on the stage. At the end of the scenario, the ceremonial guard entered the audience with a coffin to represent the deceased members of the DUI accident, and a member of the ceremonial guard played taps. The scenario had a huge impact on everyone in attendance. The sailors onstage then engaged the audience in a discussion on what it felt like to be a family member of those involved. The discussion was healthy and created an understanding of how your bad decisions would affect those you left behind. The program ended with RADM Boensel talking about the importance of our decision making at all levels. He told the sailors how much he cared about them and wanted to provide them with opportunities for success. Finally, I followed with a discussion about a visual tool that had been developed by the CSADD sailors. One was presented to everyone in attendance for their personal use.

The visual tool was an air freshener that you placed in your car's air vent, next to the ignition. On the end of the air freshener was the campaign motto, *Stop and Think.* The idea was to create a visual that would cause everyone to think about their future actions as they put their key in the car to start it: *Have you been drinking? Is driving your car the right decision? Who will I impact if I make a bad decision?* But, most importantly, that visual tool would have been given to them by leaders who had expressed concern for their well-being and wanted to provide them opportunities for success.

The training was attended by all military and civilian employees within the Navy Region Mid-Atlantic Region staff over a week. The regional safety officer stated it was the most impactful training she had seen in her twenty years of serving in her position. While leaving the auditorium, many would ask for multiple air fresheners as they wanted to place them in the cars of their children, because the message was that powerful. Thus, the impact of this group of young sailors had begun. We saw the true benefit and capability of our young sailors through inspiring them to create and implement a way to help their peers make better decisions.

Sharing and Spreading Success

I also challenged this group to establish a website and to encourage junior sailors from other commands to establish chapters throughout the region. They designed a website that communicated their Stop and Think campaign, and I started traveling around the region to spread the word and encourage leadership to support the establishment of chapters within that region. The number of chapters grew, and the social media took off. Various chapters created videos and posted them on Facebook and YouTube.

This group was *inspired* through the opportunity to impact their shipmates. They were *challenged* through the many tasks we gave them to grow their idea. Lastly, they were *empowered* to make a difference.

At this point, VADM Mark Ferguson selected me to become the fleet master chief of manpower, personnel, training, and education. After some time aboard, I presented the CSADD concept to VADM Ferguson, and the decision was made to make it a navy-wide program. On June 18, 2010, OPNAVINST 1500.80 was signed by VADM Ferguson. This instruction directed the establishment of leadership layers of support throughout regions in which chapters would register through regional offices. An annual Navy Administrative Message was released by the 21st Century Sailor office with monthly topics for the CSADD chapters to cover and promote through their own creative messaging. In 2011, the first annual CSADD Chapter of the Year program was established, and in May and June of 2012, two CSADD rallies were conducted in Norfolk and San Diego, during which CSADD sailors came together to discuss issues and share ideas while also receiving training from and having leadership discussions with senior leaders.

Enable Your People to Reach Their Full Potential

In 2013, there were over 350 CSADD chapters in navy commands around the world. Over the years CSADD has existed, the creativity and leadership skills of our young sailors have grown tremendously. They are taking ownership of many of the problems that their peer groups are often faced with. The development of videos has been so well done that in 2012, this bystander intervention video created by the CSADD chapter at Naval Station Great Lakes, led by ET3 Jon Stremmel, was utilized as navy-wide training: http://www.youtube.com/watch?v=Bzs0C3zY1O8. Naval Station Great Lakes also created the CSADD creed that can be heard in this video: http://www.youtube.com/watch?v=YWS3Av7-YsA. These young sailors created the script, wrote and performed the music, acted the parts, filmed the video with a handheld camera, and conducted all the editing on their laptops. The quality of their work was incredible. When you truly enable young people to display what they are capable of, they will always amaze you. Today, CSADD continues to thrive throughout the navy, with our young sailors leading across all peer groups. Senior leaders in the navy routinely seek them out during site visits to gain their insights.

In 2007, CSADD was an idea created by and brought to life by young sailors. Today, CSADD remains a huge part of our navy to enable success for our shipmates through developing a culture of shipmates helping shipmates. Our US Navy continues to become smaller in numbers but greater in capabilities. As we continue to get smaller, we must seek to understand the capabilities of all our people, from the oldest to the youngest. We must continue to *inspire* leaders at all levels and then *challenge* them to do more than they thought they could ever achieve while also *empowering* our young people to lead. This concept of ICE has had a tremendous impact on making our navy team stronger. Every sailor has the opportunity to lead success, and our navy gives every sailor that opportunity through the Coalition of Sailors Against Destructive Decisions.

Through the ICE concept and through CSADD, we have changed the navy-wide culture from thinking that the best approach was to teach our people only the negative outcomes of making bad decisions to now including them in the process and understanding that they can be a large part of the solution. Sometimes you have to reverse your thinking and switch from a negative perception to a positive perception to enable greater success.

As a leader, you cannot be in all places. You have to inspire, challenge, and empower others to be successful. It can sometimes be difficult to give up control. When you are struggling to do this, you may need to do some self-searching to identify what you are failing to do to grow and gain confidence in those you lead.

The following is the ICE concept as it was delivered in the sailor gram I created on this leadership topic:

ICE: Sometimes you have give up control; just chill out and let your people lead, and your goals will be achieved.

I=INSPIRE

- Be the type of leader who others will follow out of respect.
- Do the right thing all the time, even when no one is looking, and even when it does not benefit you.
- Remain focused on others' success to develop their respect and your influence.

C=CHALLENGE

- Once you can inspire others, you must challenge them.
- Help them realize their full potential.
- Enable them to see that they can do more than they ever thought possible.
- Challenge them to continue to learn. Life is a learning journey. Help them to map out their success through your confidence in them.

E=EMPOWER

- Now, empower them. You have shown confidence in them, so now, let them lead.
- As they experience leadership success, they will pursue success even more and enable your team to grow to new and amazing levels.

ICE=ChillOut

- You have now taken your leadership experience to a new level, as you have duplicated your success—all because you were able to relax, delegate, and enable a new leader to grow.
- You have *inspired*, *challenged*, and *empowered*, and those you lead will be forever grateful.

Communicating Your Concept

Sometimes the simplest of concepts enable the greatest understanding of the leadership principles you expect others to replicate. As you review the ICE concept, think about how this resonates with you. Do you have a way to effectively communicate your expectations of how your leaders need to operate? Does your approach drive a positive culture that enables success and inspires others into action? How will you ensure that the Power of Positive Leadership becomes the way of life in your organization? If you are not thinking about this, who is? You are the leader, and those you lead need to understand your expectations. In creating a positive climate for those you lead, you are growing their desire to support you in your mission. You create the culture, and the lack or level of success that you achieve is a direct result of how you inspire, challenge, and empower success for your team.

POP Points

- Never underestimate the power and impact of a small group of people willing to make a positive change for all.
- Inspire.
- Challenge.
- Empower.
- Sometimes, it can be the simplest of concepts that enable the greatest understanding of the leadership principles that you expect others to emulate.

Recommended viewing: the music video for Nickelback's "If Everyone Cared."

CHAPTER 13

It Takes Only One!

ALTHOUGH NOT INTENTIONAL, I find it fitting that this book concludes with the thirteenth chapter. As a fleet master chief in the navy, I had very high hopes that I would become the thirteenth master chief petty officer of the navy and follow my great friend and mentor, Master Chief Petty Officer of the Navy Rick West. Life can be humbling, and only one person can be selected for that particular honor. Many times, what a leader achieves after rejection may very well define his or her character. It is my hope that after this particular rejection, others take something from my actions that may inspire them to excel when they face a similar situation. Rejection can be difficult, but rejection can also be a state of mind. If you can see beyond the rejection, you may just find great opportunities. This was the situation I found myself in following my retirement from active duty as I was provided an opportunity to serve our sailors and marines.

Bob Feller Act of Valor Award Foundation

Rick West asked me to serve on a start-up nonprofit foundation called the Bob Feller Act of Valor Award Foundation. I was introduced to a great man in Peter Fertig. He—along with Rear Admiral Michael Jabaley; Bob Dibiasio, of the Cleveland Indians; Bob Arnold; and a few others—began the process of creating a foundation that would represent the three phases of Bob Feller's life. He had been a major-league baseball player, a chief petty officer in the navy (during World War II), and a member of the Baseball Hall of Fame. This became another great opportunity for me to give back to the sailors I love, as we recognize an active duty chief, a major-league baseball player, and a member of the Baseball Hall of Fame who all contribute to support our military. In the third year, we added a peer-to-peer group mentoring award, to motivate those young CSADD sailors who are also so important to me, and a senior noncommissioned officer in the marine corps award, in the name of Jerry Coleman. Had I remained on active duty, my association with this great nonprofit (www.actofvaloraward.org) would not have happened.

The Value of Our Service Members

Our men and women in uniform are amazing, and every day, they show their amazing capabilities and commitment to service—a commitment that fewer than 1 percent of our nation will ever experience. They understand the importance of showing respect for one another, they value service, and they truly value diversity as a tool that strengthens our military and our nation. It is our diversity in gender, ethnicity, backgrounds, technical skills, generations, knowledge, and so on that truly make us the greatest nation in the history of the world. Is our nation perfect? No. Is there a leader in this world who is perfect? No. In all cases, we are learning, but through valuing diversity and learning from many others, we have the greatest opportunity to grow forward as we serve others as leaders. You have probably heard the saying *there is strength in numbers*, and that is very true in most cases. However, there is greater strength in numbers when you value the diversity of your people and listen to them, and the experience they have may enable a stronger solution.

POP Is a Way of Life—Pay It Forward

Hopefully through this reading experience you have learned that the Power of Positive Leadership is more than a leadership tool. POP is a way of life. If you focus on the positive, your world will tend to be positive in response to your actions. You have the opportunity, through your actions, to pay forward a renewed and refreshing outlook on leadership execution. In today's world, the media focuses all their efforts on negative aspects. Wouldn't it be nice for once to elect the president based on who was the most positive person versus the person who drums up the most attention in the media due to their negative campaign? We need people like you, who want to lead with a positive attitude and who understand the importance of growing the next generation of leaders with a positive attitude. You have a great opportunity to learn and teach by paying POP forward through your actions.

Final Reflection and Challenge

How do you want to be perceived as a leader? This is your final question and one that I ask myself often as a reflection and an opportunity to focus my efforts on developing as a leader and for those I serve. You are the creator and retainer of your character and reputation. Only you can change your reputation. It is my hope that you take something away from my thoughts that may help you to grow as a leader and develop a positive reputation. You are the keeper of your own destiny, and only you can answer that question and shape the outcome of your leadership.

I challenge you to create a leadership-development plan for yourself that will help you to achieve your goals. Then seek others who want to do the same for themselves. I also challenge you to create a leadership vision for yourself and your team. A good friend and leader who was also a part of the USS *George Washington* leadership team was our command chaplain, Captain Robert Williams. He once shared this statement with me: "A leader's plan to achieve success is only as good as the vision that the leader develops, communicates to the team, and then commits to." Every plan must have a vision. A bad plan with a good vision performs better than a great plan without a vision.

Once again, this brings me back to a great leader, President Abraham Lincoln. His passion and vision for the Thirteenth Amendment and the need to keep the union together enabled our great nation to grow. He remained committed to his vision and ultimately accomplished his mission. The dignity of our nation grew as we began to value the life of every person, no matter their race, gender, or background.

As you talk about leadership with those you lead, always be aware that there will be naysayers. Some will always question your motivation. These types of interactions are important and enable you to make a great point when you address them head-on. Do not get discouraged by their questioning; get motivated and empowered in your answer. I will never forget a moment when I was presenting POP Leadership to a group of senior enlisted sailors at one of the major commands for our navy personnel management. One of the master chiefs stood up and asked, "Is this just another leadership concept that we have to listen to?" I was initially stunned, but I must admit, that reaction had been one of my concerns. I was concerned that others would question my motivation as to why I wanted to share leadership lessons with them, and so, I had given this some thought. My response to that master chief was that I hoped he had a leadership concept and that he was sharing it with others on his team. If so, I would really enjoy learning from him. I shared with him, as I continue to share with many, that I am a student of leadership. I also stated that it was my hope to share something with him, for him to consider to utilize in his leadership discussions with those he led. Take this concept and make it yours, if you want. More importantly, consider this: If you do not have a leadership concept to share with your people, how are you growing your team forward and to new levels of success?

Live Like You Are Dying, While Building Your Legacy

I shared with you earlier the important role that my parents played in my development. I also shared how my dad spent the last year of his life battling cancer and how, during this battle, he was also working to leave his impression on us by developing his legacy in an urgent way. My dad, Lester Francis Benning, knew that he was dying, and in his last year, he worked very diligently to ensure that we knew the impact that God had had on his life and how he had spent his life working to grow his relationship with God. He worked to complete some things that he had really hoped to complete earlier in life but couldn't, because he had been raising a family of six kids. My siblings—Cherie, Lynn, Tony, Steve, and Mike—and I all felt our dad's urgency in showing us the importance of his family to him and what contributions he had made in life by developing himself while also developing others. Of course, no one felt this more than our mom, Kathy Benning.

Our dad completed his studies and achieved his doctorate in religious studies after going years without a degree. He became an ordained minister and started to write Sunday school curriculum. He made sure that we all saw his degrees, and I still recall him sharing the location of his work with my sister. He was in the marine reserves, and he made it a point to give me a couple items from his uniform he valued from his time as a marine and that I cherish. In the last year of his life, Dad was concerned about his legacy as a dad, a leader, a minister, and a human being. He lived a life full of serving others through his service in the church and the many communities that we lived in as well as through his work to support us financially. My dad's legacy being a man of service, and in the most difficult of times, he found the greatest joy in bringing people together and serving others. That is a legacy that he gave to me and that I will always cherish.

As you review the many questions in this book to reflect on your leadership, take some time to think about your legacy in life and how you will show others what was most important to you. Take the time to communicate the importance of this throughout your life. I learned a great deal about my father in the last year of his life that I wish I would have known earlier. Of course, I have regrets about this. But these regrets have changed my actions to ensure that my family understand my family values and especially the importance of serving others.

Yes, communicating POP Leadership was my attempt to create a positive culture for the sailors who serve. More importantly, it was an attempt to initiate leadership discussions at all levels to show everyone the importance of promoting a culture of pride and success. POP alone was not going to do this, but as a good leader understanding the need to follow and complement the efforts of other leaders, POP has, in fact, had a lasting impression on those who still serve today. My dad helped me through this process, and he continues to guide me.

As I previously mentioned, Jason once stated to me, as he introduced me to the Nickelback song "If Everyone Cared," "Dad, it only takes one to change the world." Please understand that you can be that one, and I hope you improve with the Power of Positive Leadership, to make the world a better place for all those whose lives you touch, and that you pay this concept forward to have an impact on them too.

Life is a learning journey. How will you remember the destinations along the journey, and, more importantly, how will those at the many destinations remember you?

It only takes one! And you are the one to pay POP forward.

Scott's Leadership Library

Lincoln on Leadership, by Donald T. Phillips
Whale Done! by Ken Blanchard
The Winning Attitude, by John C. Maxwell
Developing the Leaders Around You, by John C. Maxwell
Becoming a Person of Influence, by John C. Maxwell
The 360 Degree Leader, by John C. Maxwell
Our Iceberg Is Melting, by John Kotter
The 5 Levels of Leadership, by John C. Maxwell
The Power Behind Positive Thinking, by Eric Fellman
The Leader's Compass, by Ed Ruggero and Dennis Haley
How Successful People Think, by John C. Maxwell
The Power of Leadership, by John C. Maxwell
The Oz Principle, by Roger Connors, Tom Smith, and Craig Hickman
The Mentor Leader, by Tony Dungy
Appreciative Leadership, by Diana Whitney, Amanda Trosten-Bloom, and Kae Rader
Winning with People, by John C. Maxwell
Your Leadership Legacy, by Robert M. Galford and Regina Fazio Maruca
The FISH Series:

FISH!, by Stephen C. Lundin, Harry Paul, and John Christensen
FISH! Tales, by John Christensen, Stephen C. Lundin, and Harry Paul
FISH! Sticks, by Harry Paul, John Christensen, and Stephen C. Lundin
FISH! For Life, by Harry Paul, John Christensen, and Stephen C. Lundin

Catch!, By Cyndi Crother
Good to Great, by Jim Collins
The Leadership Secrets of Collin Powell, by Oren Harari
The Radical Leap, by Steve Farber
The Heart of a Leader, by Ken Blanchard
The Right to Lead, by John C. Maxwell
Encouragement Changes Everything, by John. C. Maxwell
Teamwork Makes the Dream Work, by John C. Maxwell
Positive Leadership, by Mike Magee
Dare to Dream, by John C. Maxwell
Go for Gold, by John C. Maxwell
The Servant Leader, by Ken Blanchard and Phil Hodges
The 21 Irrefutable Laws of Leadership, by John C. Maxwell
The Dream Manager, by Matthew Kelly
The Power of Nice, by Linda Kaplan Thaler and Robin Koval
Everyone Communicates, Few Connect, by John C. Maxwell
Great Quotes from Great Leaders, by Peggy Anderson
Leadership Is an Art, by Max Depree
The 12 Leadership Principles of Dean Smith, by David Chadwick
Leadership and Self-Deception, by Arbinger Institute
101 Ways to Improve Your Communication Skills Instantly, by Jon Condrill
Who Moved My Cheese?, by Spencer Johnson
The One Minute Manager, by Ken Blanchard and Spencer Johnson
What Would Lincoln Do?, by David Acord
Full Speed Ahead, by Joyce Weiss
Switch, by Chip Heath and Dan Heath
Made to Stick, by Chip Heath and Dan Heath
Tipping Point, by Malcolm Gladwell
Execution, by Larry Bossidy and Ram Charan
All In, by Paula Broadwell
Leaders Without Borders, by Doug Dickerson
Discover the Greatness in You, by Milton Willis and Michael Willis
Lessons for Success, by Lorraine A. Darconte

Make Today Count, by John C. Maxwell
Leadership 101, by John C. Maxwell
Mentoring 101, by John C. Maxwell
Success 101, by John C. Maxwell
Attitude 101, by John C. Maxwell
The 17 Essential Qualities of a Team Player, by John C. Maxwell
I'm Not the Boss, I Just Work Here, by Howard Jonas
Great Leaders Grow, by Ken Blanchard and Mark Miller
The Wit and Wisdom of Benjamin Franklin, by Barnes and Noble
Lincoln Stories for Leaders, by Donald T. Phillips
B2B Means "Back to Basics," by Dr. Bill Quain
Appreciative Inquiry, by David Cooperrider and Diana Whitney
Gently Down the Stream, by Mat Weinstein and Luke Barber
Blink, by Malcolm Gladwell
Outliers, by Malcolm Gladwell
Washington's Farewell, by Stuart Murray
Every Day a Friday, by Joel Osteen
The Seven Habits of Highly Effective People, by Stephen R. Covey
The 8th Habit, by Stephen R. Covey
The Speed of Trust, by Stephen R. Covey
Today Matters, by John C. Maxwell
The Power of Positive Confrontation, by Barbara Pachter and Susan Magee
A Leader's Heart, by John C. Maxwell
The First 90 Days, by Michael Watkins
In Harm's Way, by Doug Stanton
Be All You Can Be, by John C. Maxwell
The Serving Leader, by Ken Jennings and John Stahl-Wert
Leadership Smarts, by Ken Blanchard
The Maxwell Daily Reader, by John C. Maxwell
Fred Factor, by Mark Sanborn
Empowerment Takes a Minute, by Ken Blanchard
High Five!, by Ken Blanchard and Sheldon Bowles
The Present, by Spencer Johnson

Leadership, by William Safire and Leonard Afir
Leading Quietly, by Joseph L. Badaracco
The Power of Alignment, by George Labovitz and Victor Rosansky
Who Says Elephants Can't Dance?, by Louis V. Gerstner
Money Ball, by Michael Lewis
Common Sense Leadership, by Roger Fulton
Common Sense Supervision, by Roger Fulton
How Full Is Your Bucket?, by Tom Rath and Donald O. Clifton
The Leadership Pipeline, by Ram Charan, Stephen Drotter, and James Noel
George Washington on Leadership, by Richard Brookhiser
The Bowden Way, by Bobby Bowden
The Power of Ethical Management, by Ken Blanchard and Norman Vincent Peale
The Wit and Wisdom of Abraham Lincoln, by Anthony Gross
The Last Lecture, by Randy Pauseh
Soldier: The Life of Colin Powell, by Karen DeYoung
Leadership Gold, by John C. Maxwell
The Hamster Revolution, by Mike Song, Vicki Halsey, and Tim Burress
Just Be Honest, by Steven Gaffney
25 Ways to Win with People, by John C. Maxwell and Les Parrot
The Other Side of the Card, by Mike Morrison
A Leader's Legacy, by James Kouzes and Barry Posner
Inspire! What Great Leaders Do, by Lance Secretan
Gung Ho!, by Ken Blanchard and Sheldon Bowles
Raving Fans, by Ken Blanchard and Sheldon Bowles
Speak to Win, by Brian Tracy
The Leadership Pill, by Ken Blanchard and Marc Muchnick
You Don't Need a Title to Be a Leader, by Mark Sanborn
The Nature of Leadership, by B. Joseph White and Yaron Prywes
Attitude Is Everything, by Jeff Keller
The Five Pillars of Leadership, by Paul J. Meyer and Randy Slechta
The Power of I Am, by Joel Osteen

APPENDIX B

Reflection Questions

CREATE A REFLECTION ledger. Each day, write one of the following questions in your ledger, and then answer them, documenting the various responses. Also, consider reading this book with your team and creating reflection ledgers together so that you can discuss all your answers. Watch the entire team succeed as you share your experiences and develop your communication, understanding, and trust.

1) Life is a learning journey on which you will pass through many destinations. How will you remember the destinations, and how will those at these destinations remember you?

2) Are you smiling, and are you ready to start your day by having a positive impact on those you lead and follow, or will you just walk by them? How will you do this?

3) Have you ever smiled at someone and taken notice of what occurred in response? Make a note of how it changed that person's demeanor.

4) What does pride projection mean to you, as a leader?

5) How do you get those you lead to understand your thought process through means other than your verbal communications?

6) What did your mentors see in you, and how did they inspire your confidence in your own ability? How do you pay this forward?

7) Are you satisfied that you are the type of leader you want your team members to replicate? If not, what can you do to improve?

8) How do you expect those who work for you, your peers, and those you work for to deal with specific situations? Are you setting the example that they need to emulate? How can you improve in this area?

9) What will your leadership legacy look like? How successful was your team after you left them?

10) How do other people see you? How can you improve their perception of you?

11) Have you ever had a boss or coworker who, when having a bad day, would turn it into a bad day for everyone else too? How can you help that person understand their impact on others?

12) Would you want to be influenced by an apparently negative person? Why or why not?

13) When you wake up in the morning, how do you react? Do you wake up thinking; *I'm going to have a great day today*? If not, should you?

14) Can you imagine someone in your life telling you how you need to improve? How well would you accept their advice?

15) Take a look around you. How many spirits are being uplifted through people going to work and making money? How can you influence a positive change in their lives?

16) Will they still be able to respect you after you tackle a negative situation with them?

17) Positivity is infectious, and so is negativity. Which one will you project, and which one will your organization's climate reflect? How will you tackle this?

18) How do you educate your followers to be responsible so that they can remain a productive and successful member of your team?

19) Which do you want your team to emulate, success or failure? Which are you projecting through your actions, and which are you presenting while preparing them for their future? Consider examples of how you can work on this.

20) When you sought out other leaders for guidance, did you ask them how they failed or how they succeeded?

21) Have you ever thought about how we, as individuals, start to develop influencing behaviors? You are not born a leader. How can you guide your children to become a good one?

22) Do you lead those you work for? How do you influence your leaders?

23) When you became a member of some type of team, maybe a sports or academic team, did you just sit back and let everyone else tell you what to do? Or did you adapt to make the team stronger and ensure that they understood your point of view?

24) If you ever had a negative leader who did not want to listen to you, did you want to stay on his or her team or move on to another one? Give an example of this.

25) If you ever had a coach who yelled at you all the time for doing something wrong, and who never invested in you by teaching you how to do something better, did you enjoy that experience? How did you respond to the situation then, and how would you respond today?

26) Think about the influencers in your life and how they have shaped you. Are you applying what you have learned to your own goals and priorities so that you can have greater satisfaction in your life? How have you done so, and how do you plan to continue to do so?

27) What brings the most joy to your life? Make a list of activities and think about how often you do them. Should you do them more often? If so, start scheduling the time.

28) Are you where you need to be today? How can you better serve your interests?

29) How many times have you seen someone depart a job as they were deemed unable to adapt to change? Give an example of this, and make a note on what you could have done or will do to support such people.

30) Did you wake up with a positive attitude and the desire to promote a positive environment for those around you?

31) Did you begin your day with the goal of helping others to grow and succeed? How can you make personal changes to ensure that you do the same?

32) Did you do all that you could today to give your very best to those you serve as a leader? How can you improve so that you are better for them tomorrow?

33) What standards are they working to emulate? The ones you are discussing or the ones you are modeling? Review the last couple of weeks and think about situations where you could have modeled more or better.

34) Do you have a daily "hooyah" moment with your team? How can you motivate your team to create one?

35) Do you bring teams together and encourage teamwork to enable their success? Consider where you can break down barriers and build bridges for your team, and make a list.

36) How do you work to develop trust with those you are serving as a leader? How do you consider doing it with every member of your team? Make a list and think of different ways for all of them.

37) Do you share your experiences with others to build trust and influence? What experiences have you shared so far? Were they effective?

38) Take a look at your organization. Are some relationships weak and in need of work? Can you break down some of the barriers and begin to rebuild the trust so that you can once again influence the entire team's success?

39) How can you engage a group who seem to be the problem and make them become part of the solution? Develop a strategy to do just that.

40) Do you have a way to effectively communicate your expectations for how your leaders operate? Bring your team together and develop a list of expectations that everyone can accept.

41) Does your approach to leadership promote a positive culture that inspires others to action and enables their success? Where can you improve, and how can you communicate better?

42) How do you ensure that the Power of Positive (POP) Leadership becomes a way of life in your organization? Develop a plan for how you can increase awareness of the concept and communicate it in a manner that will convince your team to accept it.

43) How do you want to be perceived as a leader? Write down your thoughts and then consider making a focused effort to increase your awareness of how others perceive you.

44) If you do not have a leadership concept to share with your people, how will you help them to improve? Develop your own concept or pick one from POP Leadership and make it your own—or better yet, convince your team to buy into one and have them help you with it.

45) Life is a learning journey on which you will pass through many destinations. How will you remember the destinations, and how will those at these destinations remember you? How can you improve your attitude and approach so that you leave a lasting positive impression on those you engage along your journey?

About the Author

Scott A. Benning
Retired Fleet Master Chief, US Navy

SCOTT JOINED THE navy at age seventeen and thus began his thirty-year military career, in which he rose to become one of the top five enlisted sailors for the entire US Navy.

He started as a logistics specialist, and his tours included the following: Naval Ocean Processing Facility Dam Neck, Virginia Beach, Virginia; USS *Comte de Grasse* (DD 974), Norfolk, Virginia; Underwater Construction Team One, Little Creek, Virginia; USS *Gunston Hall* (LSD 44), Little Creek, Virginia; Norfolk Naval Shipyard, Portsmouth, Virginia; and USS *Detroit* (AOE 4), Earl, New Jersey. His command leadership tours included Fighter Squadron One Zero Three (VF 103), Oceana, Virginia; Carrier Air Wing Seventeen (CVW 17), Oceana, Virginia; USS *George Washington* (CVN 73), Norfolk, Virginia; Naval Station Norfolk, Norfolk, Virginia; and Navy Region Mid-Atlantic, Norfolk, Virginia.

In 2009, Scott was selected as the fleet master chief of manpower, personnel, training, and education, and as such led and served over three hundred thousand sailors around the world. During his time, as fleet master chief, he was best known for his development of the Power of Positive Leadership and as the founder of the Coalition of Sailors Against Destructive Decisions (CSADD). He also served as senior enlisted leader for the secretary of defense's Comprehensive Review Working Group to review the Don't Ask, Don't Tell policy, which resulted in the Report of the Comprehensive Review of the Issues Associated with a Repeal of "Don't Ask, Don't Tell" going to congress.

Scott completed his thirty years of naval service in March 2013. In July 2013 he entered into government service as a member of the Department of the Navy Sexual Assault Prevention and Response office in Washington D.C. He now resides in Stafford, Virginia, with his wife of thirty-three years, Cheryl Lynn Taylor Benning. Both of their sons serve in the US Navy: the older one, Scott "Anthony" Jr., as a navy civilian director of fitness, sports, and aquatics at Naval Station Norfolk and the younger one, Jason Christopher, as a navy surface warfare officer in Riverine Squadron Four, Little Creek, Virginia.

Scott is a graduate of the Navy Senior Enlisted Academy and the University of North Carolina's Navy Corporate Business Course; in 2008, he also graduated from Southern Illinois University with a Bachelor of Science degree in workforce education and development. He was a founding member of the Bob Feller Act of Valor Award Foundation's board of directors and has served in many other volunteer positions throughout his career.

His military awards include the Legion of Merit, three Meritorious Service Medals, three Navy Commendation Medals, three Navy Achievement Medals, two Meritorious Unit Commendations, seven

Good Conduct Medals, two National Defense Service Medals, two Armed Forces Expeditionary Medals, an Armed Forces Service Medal, and a NATO Medal, among other service decorations.

If you enjoyed this book, please cut out the referrals below and give them to friends or coworkers so that they too can order the book and benefit from POP Leadership.

The Power of Positive Leadership
Scott A. Benning
Available from Amazon.com and other retailers
(Printed by CreateSpace, An Amazon.com Company)

The Power of Positive Leadership
Scott A. Benning
Available from Amazon.com and other retailers
(Printed by CreateSpace, An Amazon.com Company)

The Power of Positive Leadership
Scott A. Benning
Available from Amazon.com and other retailers
(Printed by CreateSpace, An Amazon.com Company)

The Power of Positive Leadership
Scott A. Benning
Available from Amazon.com and other retailers
(Printed by CreateSpace, An Amazon.com Company)

Made in the USA
San Bernardino, CA
11 April 2017